# Nutritional Treatments <u>to</u> Improve Mental Health Disorders

Non-Pharmaceutical Interventions for Depression, Anxiety, Bipolar & ADHD

Anne Procyk, ND

Published by
PESI Publishing & Media
PESI, Inc.
3839 White Ave.
Eau Claire, WI 54703

Cover: Amy Rubenzer
Editing: Marietta Whittlesey
Layout: Amy Rubenzer, Bookmasters

ISBN: 9781683731610
All Rights Reserved.
Printed in the United States of America

PESI
Publishing
& Media
www.publishing.pesi.com

# Contents

## Beyond DSM-5: Functional Medicine to Understand and Treat the Underlying Cause

## The Physical Basis of Mental Health: Sleep, Activity, and Food

## Specific Nutrient Deficiencies that Commonly Contribute to Mental Health Symptoms

## Putting it all Together: Functional Medicine Diagnoses

## Find and Treat the Cause: The Questions to Answer, Organized by Diagnosis

SECTION 3

SECTION 4

SECTION 5

# About The Author

 **Dr. Anne Procyk** is a naturopathic physician and the founder of Third Stone Health, an integrative health center in Essex, Connecticut. She has been practicing as an integrative primary care physician for two decades, seeing thousands of patients and developing a keen understanding of the complex relationships between physical and mental health. In addition to serving her busy practice, she currently teaches seminars nationwide on "Nutrition and Integrative Strategies for Mental Health Disorders."

## Philosophy

I decided to become a naturopathic physician because I wanted to understand how people work: physically, mentally, emotionally, and spiritually. How the biochemistry and physiology of the human body yield the emergent qualities of consciousness and soul fascinates me. How intangibles like thoughts and emotions can instantly trigger measurable physical responses never ceases to amaze me.

Science has yielded a tremendous amount of knowledge, but the practice of medicine requires a constant discipline to understand more deeply how to apply that knowledge for the benefit of one unique individual—our patient.

To truly address a person's needs requires effective communication and understanding of underlying causes. I am honored by the opportunity to work with people at all stages of health, and feel eternally grateful for the ability to help people transform their lives through improved health.

## Education

Dr. Anne Procyk earned her doctorate at National College of Naturopathic Medicine and graduated *cum laude* from Carleton College with degrees in chemistry and medical ethics. She is a member of the American Association of Naturopathic Physicians, the Connecticut Naturopathic Physicians Association, and the Association for the Advancement of Restorative Medicine. She is also a founding board member of Autism Families CONNECTicut, a non-profit organization committed to providing social and recreational opportunities for children and families affected by autism.

# Introduction

What I find most exciting in my work is witnessing just how dramatically someone can blossom, at any age and even after years of suffering, when his/her brain chemistry comes into balance. Real people, such as the mom who had first attempted suicide as a teenager and had been on psychiatric meds ever since, who was able to get off her meds, and asked, "Is this what normal people feel like?" Her teenage daughter, who was starting to show similar symptoms, who brightened up and never experienced that kind of suffering, not only because her mother was healthier, but because early intervention with special nutrition prevented the negative effects of their genetic anomaly. The teenage boy with ADHD who said, "I never knew I could be *good* at school!" The middle-aged woman with bipolar who had spent her life in and out of the hospital who got her first job, and held it, for years, still counting. And the precocious 10-year-old boy whose angry tantrums and outbursts defied a clean diagnosis, who had been worsened by pharmaceutical therapy, and who still struggled to cope with his emotions despite years of therapy, who said, "The tools in my toolbox work now!"

These stories are the hope of every person who has ever taken or been recommended a psychiatric medication. But all too often, the effects of medications fall short. In those cases we need to dig deeper and treat *all* the roots of the problem. Clinicians sometimes ask me, "How do I convince someone to eat healthily when they have the option to just take a pill?" My answer is, "If the pill is working as well as they want it to, tell them to thank their lucky stars. If it is not, and they want to feel better than they do, help them address the issues that there is no pill to fix." **This book will teach you how and why to address those fundamentals necessary for peak brain function and optimal mental and emotional health.** Included are references for resources to help educate your clients, as well as tools and strategies for helping your clients experience firsthand how powerful these therapies are.

This information is the culmination of 20 years of work with patients. When I first entered the world of medicine, I was told to choose my specialty. Did I want to treat people's minds, or their bodies? At that moment I realized I simply could not choose, because their functions are inseparable. So I chose a third path—learning how to navigate the vast complexities of the mind-body connections. Very quickly, I learned that integrating therapies from different specialties to provide truly comprehensive medicine for clients required not just a team approach, but a whole new way of understanding health and disease.

Most often, when mental health clinicians hear the term "mind-body" medicine, what they think of first are various forms of meditations and mindfulness techniques. And indeed, these are very powerful therapies, supported by research showing some of the fascinating ways these techniques alter the physical state of the body. But the "mind-body connection" is a two-way street, and just as people can alter their neurochemistry through meditation, people can also alter their mood, focus, and cognition by addressing physical issues.

In an ideal world, these issues should have been addressed before a person was ever given a mental health diagnosis or prescribed a psychiatric medication, since nearly every diagnosis in the *Diagnostic and Statistical Manual of Mental Disorders (5th ed.)* (American Psychiatric Association, 2013) shares one common criterion: organic causes of the symptoms must be ruled out. Yet this is the one criterion that is most likely overlooked, or only minimally investigated. The result: **Millions of people unnecessarily suffer painful mental health symptoms due to untreated nutrient deficiencies, hormonal imbalances, blood sugar swings, and excess inflammation.** Psychiatric medications can and do help many people, but many of the most fundamental imbalances that cause mental health symptoms are caused by issues that medication cannot fix. **To help someone truly feel and function at their best, all the different aspects of health must be thoroughly addressed.**

You may be the first clinician your clients have encountered who addresses these fundamentals and helps them finally break out of this vicious cycle of disease and dysfunction and truly reach their potential. Some people at this point jump to the conclusion that the person was misdiagnosed. In some cases, this is certainly true. There are some obvious cases, such as the stories I hear from addictions counselors who report that most of their patients get diagnosed with bipolar because they are evaluated while under the influence. The DSM-5 has attempted to clarify when these different diagnoses should be used, but confusion still remains.

But more commonly, it is not that obvious. Every day I see people diagnosed with bipolar caused by hormonal imbalance, depression that is being caused by a nutritional deficiency, ADHD caused by blood sugar imbalance, and anxiety that results from excess inflammation. But it's not so simple that every case of depression is caused by a nutritional deficiency—some people suffer depression because of hormonal imbalance, some because of excess inflammation, and some for all of the above reasons. Sometimes blood sugar imbalances cause anxiety, without any ADHD symptoms, and sometimes excess inflammation causes bipolar, without any anxiety. Different combinations of nutritional deficiencies can result in any and all of these diagnoses. And of course, many people suffer from more than one diagnosis, and those diagnoses may or may not share an underlying cause. So how do you figure out what is going on?

The key is asking the right questions. I have been asked many times, in different ways, "How can I tell if it's ADHD or a nutritional deficiency?" But this question misses the point entirely. If the person meets the criteria for ADHD, clearly there is a problem that needs to be addressed, and ADHD accurately and succinctly describes what the person is experiencing. But "ADHD" as a diagnosis is just a description: It reveals nothing about the critical question, which is, "*Why* does this person suffer the symptoms of ADHD?" It might be a nutritional deficiency. It might be poor blood sugar regulation. It might both. It may also include aspects of physiology and neurochemistry we do not yet understand. **But only when we ask what is causing a person's symptoms can we start to unravel the complex biology underlying how someone feels and know what interventions will help.**

This approach, called *functional medicine*, is a different, and in some ways radically new, approach to medicine. It requires breaking out of the model that assumes that each diagnosis has one cause and therefore one treatment. Chronic disease, both mental and physical, much more commonly arises when multiple issues start to cause a positive feedback loop, more commonly known as a "vicious cycle." True healing requires breaking these vicious cycles of disease by addressing *all* the different causes of disease in the appropriate order.

## How to Use This Book

**Section 1** will introduce you to this new model of medicine called *functional medicine*. New therapies are exciting, but all too often when a new therapy is publicized, it gets applied in inappropriate ways or incorrect situations, and then it fails to work. For any therapy to be effective, it is critical to understand the principles on which it is based. Section 1 will lay the foundation on which the therapies in Section 2 build. It can be tempting to jump straight to the hands-on application of the material, but neglecting Section 1 will compromise your ability to most effectively apply the therapies you will learn in Sections 2, 3, and 4.

**Section 2** will explain the physical basis of mental health: all the basic essentials without which the brain cannot function. Every single one of your clients needs all of these issues to be addressed to be able to function at their best. The possible problems are as diverse as the population you serve, but these are the issues most critical to deal with. No medications exist which can compensate for not addressing these basic issues, and yet "jumping to the pill" is too often the approach taken in our current medical climate, by both patients and doctors.

**Section 3** will expand further on certain critical nutrients that are commonly deficient, and that deficiency results in mental health symptoms. All nutrients are important, for both mental health and physical health, but knowing the most common deficiencies, what symptoms they cause, how to assess them, and how to address them will further refine your ability to help educate and motivate clients.

**Section 4** has two main focuses: The first will delve deeper into the physiology of how issues disrupt mental and emotional balance. These diagnoses will often require referrals to specialists to completely address, and knowing when and how to refer is another way you can help your patients get the most effective treatments. Understanding these diagnoses is not essential, and outside the scope of practice for many mental health clinicians, but many people prefer to be familiar with these subjects because they further explain why all the therapies in Section 2 are so important.

Then I will pull together all of the previous information and organize it by major diagnosis. As clinicians, it is critically important to remember to treat people, not diagnoses. But it is the diagnosis, or diagnoses, that help us know what questions to start asking to understand why a person suffers the diagnosis they do. This section will guide you through the questions to ask to determine which therapies are ones necessary for each individual person.

## Every Effective Therapy Has Value

**With the help of the information and tools in this book, you can integrate these therapies into your practice, along with the powerful therapies you already use.** I can't emphasize enough the value of true integrative medicine; every effective therapy has value, but no single therapy, or even a single approach to medicine, is the complete answer for every person or every situation. But when we as clinicians learn from each other, and bring together the best of all worlds of medicine, both in our own practices and via referrals and team approaches, the effect can be synergistic. Using the therapies in this book will help people's brains function better, and when their brains function better, they are more capable of responding to the other therapies you already use. What I hope you experience as you incorporate these fundamentals into your practice is that you witness your clients benefiting not only from these therapies directly, but also benefiting more quickly and more deeply to the therapies you already use.

# Beyond the DSM-5®

Functional Medicine to Understand and
Treat the Underlying Cause

SECTION 1

# Functional Medicine: A New Way of Approaching Health, Disease, Diagnosis, and Treatment

*Functional medicine* is a new way of approaching the very concepts of health, disease, diagnosis, and treatment. The easiest way to introduce this concept of functional medicine is with a simple, familiar example: high blood pressure. An easy measurement identifies if a person's blood pressure is high, and there's no room for debate on what the numbers are. But different doctors will respond to those numbers differently. Most people are familiar with how the conventional doctor responds: by prescribing a medication to lower blood pressure and having the person return in several weeks to verify the medication is working, effectively lowering the person's blood pressure into the normal range.

**However, a doctor of functional medicine is going to take a different approach.** Instead of jumping to prescribing a medication, the doctor will first examine all the different factors that can elevate blood pressure, and determine if any of them are a problem in this particular patient. The doctor of functional medicine will also examine all the different ways the body regulates blood pressure, to determine if the source of the problem is there. This process involves evaluating many different potential issues: nutritional factors, environmental factors, stress factors, and internal physiological factors such as inflammation, hormones, and blood sugar. Even a simple diagnosis like high blood pressure requires looking at a variety of factors that could potentially be causing the problem.

In the world of mental health diagnosis, where, of course, the diagnoses are much more complex and manifest in a variety of different ways, the approach is still the same. The doctor examines all the different factors that can cause depression, or bipolar, or ADHD, and then determines what the underlying causes are for each unique case.

Determining if a person has depression, or bipolar, or other diagnoses is much more involved, and harder, than simply checking blood pressure. But that process also serves as the first step of identifying underlying issues that functional medicine can treat to correct the problem. **There are three important points to remember as you learn more about this process:**

1. There is almost always more than one underlying cause.

2. Each case will have a different combination of underlying causes.

3. People with the same diagnosis may need different treatments.

Only rarely is there just one issue that is causing all of a person's symptoms. All patients, and practitioners, would love to find that "magic bullet" cure that will fix all of a person's symptoms, quickly and forever. Only rarely is that possible. Usually, by the time a person's symptoms have progressed to the point of receiving a diagnosis, there are multiple factors causing the problem. Even after identifying one issue that is causing a problem, the doctor needs to continue looking for other issues to truly understand the whole problem and how all the different factors influence each other.

Because diagnoses arise from a combinations of causative factors, each person is unique. It does not take long in practice to learn that even people with the same diagnosis can experience their symptoms in dramatically different ways. These sub-types within the major diagnosis categories exist because there are so many different potential combinations of causes for symptoms. These differences provide clues to help the doctor identify the underlying causes in each unique individual.

**Because people with the same diagnosis have different causes of their symptoms, they will need different combinations of treatments.** Back to the very simple example of high blood pressure: One person may need to address a nutritional deficiency, whereas one person may need to learn to handle stress more effectively, and yet another person may need to balance inflammation. Each of these people will need different treatments, and all of those treatments will correct high blood pressure when used for the right person.

The other side of this fact is that even though a treatment may help one person with high blood pressure, it may *not* help another person with high blood pressure whose reason for having high blood pressure is completely different. The treatment always has to be customized to the person, and knowing which treatment is going to help requires knowing what the underlying cause is. Again, in the world of mental health where the diagnoses are so much more complex, this fundamental approach becomes that much more important.

## Working With Clients at a Deeper Level: Transforming Medical Care into Health Care

This process of functional diagnosis and more personalized treatment plans requires working with patients at a much deeper level. This deeper connection is what so many patients and practitioners are truly looking for: the shift from *medical care* to *health care.*

The United States currently has a medical system consisting of a network of people and places (doctors, nurses, physical therapists, psychotherapists, paramedics, hospitals, offices, community clinics, urgent care centers, and visiting nurses) who help people who are sick or injured. But so often the term "health care" is used instead because I believe most people truly want a health care system: a network of people and places that not only helps people who are sick or injured, but also works with people to improve their health, ideally reaching optimum health.

Helping people reach optimum health requires working with people even after the crisis has been resolved. It requires not just helping people with the immediate issues, but educating them about how to further improve health. Education is not always easy—just as a child doesn't learn math facts by looking at sheet of multiplication tables once, rarely do people learn how to eat, sleep, or exercise well just from reading a handout once. Education requires engagement and effort, from both the student and the teacher. Typically, it will take repeated effort; a child usually has to practice math facts many times in the process of learning them. But the process itself is rewarding, and the result is priceless. Optimal health yields higher functioning, a greater level of happiness, and the ability to prevent some diseases.

Working at this deeper level does not mean that "quick-fix" strategies should be thrown out. **On the contrary, medications and psychotherapy strategies that provide relief are extremely valuable. These tools will always be an essential part of practice.** The difference between medical care and health care is to understand that these strategies are not the end, but only the beginning. People will see the most improvement when practitioners continue to work with them to improve their health, even after the crisis has been resolved. While not all people are looking for this level of support, many are, and both the patient and practitioner benefit. The patient achieves a higher level of functioning, self-awareness, and happiness. The practitioner feels an increased satisfaction at having facilitated a deeper level of healing.

Despite the enormous reward, both patients and practitioners can still be easily seduced by the promise of the quick fix. And many of the strategies in this book can create significant improvement over a short period of time. But because almost everyone will need more than one strategy to truly feel their best, it is important to avoid the mind-set of sifting through the information to find the one thing that applies to a given person or situation. To truly maximize potential, it is important to go through the full process. Celebrate and enjoy each success along the way, but continue working at deeper levels to truly achieve optimal health.

## Transcending the Mind-Body Separation

The world of medicine still typically divides disease into two categories: physical illness and mental illness. But the brain is not separate from the body, and the body is not separate from the brain. All parts of the body are one living organism, and a tremendous amount of research has been done showing an enormous number ways that each can affect the other. Looking at these connections requires not just psychiatry, but every specialty in medicine. Issues with neurology, endocrinology, gastroenterology, cardiology, and immunology all directly impact brain function and how a person feels and thinks. Psychoneuroimmunology is the field of research that specifically studies these connections with the goal of fully understanding how they work. There is still an immense amount more to learn about all those connections.

While psychotherapists are quite familiar with this concept, commonly, lay people are not. The fact that physical health affects mental health and mental health affects physical health is still a new concept for many people. Therefore teaching people who suffer from mental illness that it is *not* "all in their head" can be an extremely empowering concept. It also opens the door to working with many therapies that are so often overlooked when both the patient and doctor focus strictly on the mental-emotional symptoms.

Even people who are quite comfortable with this concept often still overlook so many of the ways that the mind-body connection is a two-way street. Every parent has experienced the change in mood an infant has when tired. These changes won't be the same for every child. One child may feel sad more easily and be prone to crying, while another may feel more irritable and be more prone to yelling, but every child changes in a noticeable way. Yet the parent may be completely unaware of how their own sleep deprivation is affecting their mood, causing symptoms of depression, or anxiety, or irritability.

Because these relationships between mind and body are not identical in each person, they can be hard to identify. Some people will use that fact to argue that the relationships simply do not exist. But to really understand health and disease, all relationships need to be examined. And to help a given individual, uncovering the nature of the relationship between how he/she feels, how he/she thinks, and all the different nutrition and environmental factors that affect brain function is critical.

## What Really Causes Neurochemical Imbalances?

The complexity of how the mind and body are connected is vast. The dominant model, "neurochemical imbalances," has been used for the last several decades to explain many of these connections. This model has yielded both tremendous progress and benefits, but also significant negative effects. To use this model most effectively, it is important to understand both what it does well, as well as what it cannot do.

**The biggest benefit of this model is that it provides a framework to explain some of the mind-body connections.** When a certain neurotransmitter is out of balance or not responding, the results are changes in mood and cognitive function. Understanding how these neurotransmitters function and the roles they play is incredibly powerful. This understanding has helped to lessen the stigma of mental illness as simply a "character flaw." When people learn that there really is a physiological basis for how they feel, somehow it turns into a more tangible problem. The most dramatic tangible result of understanding some of these neurotransmitter relationships is the development of a number of drugs that powerfully alter these neurotransmitters, affecting both mood and cognition. These drugs can and do significantly improve quality of life for many people.

But there are also some negative effects of this chemical imbalance model. In my opinion, the biggest and most widespread negative effect is that our medical system has come to have an over-reliance on drug therapy. Any and every intervention needs to be applied to the correct situation. Knowing which intervention is appropriate requires a thorough assessment of the situation. But in the current medical climate of short office visits and seeing a different doctor on each visit, so often that deeper assessment gets neglected. People say no more than a few sentences about feeling down, stressed, anxious, or having trouble sleeping, and a few minutes later the doctor prescribes a selective serotonin reuptake inhibitor (SSRI), an anti-anxiety medication, or a sleeping aid. There will always be situations where those medications are needed and helpful, but when they are prescribed before really analyzing the situation, there is greater risk of people being prescribed medications they do not actually need.

When people are prescribed medications they don't need, there is much greater risk of negative reactions and side effects to the medication, which then create additional problems. There is also the more insidious problem of the patient not receiving the intervention that is most appropriate and helpful for the situation. If a person is feeling anxious and having difficulty because they are living in an abusive relationship, simply medicating the anxiety with a drug is not addressing the cause of the problem. The person needs therapy and other forms of support to end the abuse.

Another potential negative effect of using the chemical imbalance model is how frequently it is misinterpreted. When people hear the term "chemical imbalance," most often they interpret it as a biological inevitability, something they have no power to change, and that they simply need to learn to live with or take a drug to manage the symptoms. But even though chemical imbalances may explain *how* someone is feeling their symptoms, it never explains *why*.

For example, low serotonin will cause depression. But identifying that serotonin is low does not explain *why* it is low. **The key to understanding someone's depression is understanding why the serotonin is low, not just giving an SSRI to make the serotonin last longer.** The problem did not start with a Prozac deficiency! Prozac can help, but identifying why it is needed is key to figuring out what the real cure is. Maybe the person is protein deficient, and therefore cannot make serotonin. In that case, eating protein will eliminate the need for Prozac. Maybe the person is eicosapentaenoic acid (EPA) deficient and therefore the serotonin receptors are not responding appropriately, so the serotonin cannot reach the intended target. In that case, eating more EPA would eliminate the need for Prozac. Maybe the person is eating a healthy diet, including both protein and EPA, but has digestive issues that prevent the body from absorbing those nutrients. In that case, correcting the digestive issues would eliminate the need for medication. **These are all examples of how digging deeper to identify the true cause of the chemical imbalance can potentially *cure* the problem rather than continuing to manage the problem.**

## Beyond Complementary and Alternative Medicine: Functional, Integrative Medicine

Sometimes various parts of this approach are referred to as "complementary medicine" or "alternative medicine." But these words, particularly "alternative," imply an either/or approach. To continue using the example from the last section, sometimes people (both doctors and patients) think of using nutrition "instead" of a pharmaceutical medication to treat depression. "If the drug doesn't work, I'll try something else." But that kind of thinking misses the two most important questions: "What are the underlying causes of a person's symptoms?" and "What are the most effective ways to addresses those underlying issues?" The functional medicine approach answers the first question, and integrative medicine takes the best of all forms of medicine to treat those issues as effectively as possible.

Functional medicine, or asking, "What is causing this person's symptoms?" is independent of a patient's type of issues or a practitioner's specialty. Psychotherapists and physical therapists can both take this approach. Psychiatrists and gastroenterologists may, or may not, take this approach. It can be applied to any problem in any kind of medicine, and the most thorough practitioners of any specialty will use this approach. Because this approach is so rare in medicine, it has really become its own specialty.

**Integrative medicine simply means bringing together any and all necessary treatments.** Because there are almost always multiple underlying causes by the time someone's symptoms are severe enough to be diagnosed with depression, anxiety, bipolar, or ADHD, most often more than one treatment is necessary to help some function at their best. Psychotherapists are quite familiar with how a drug can never have the same effect as psychotherapy, and psychotherapy can never substitute for a needed medication. Each treats a different aspect of the problem, and to try to use one in place of the other simply does not make sense.

Equally familiar is witnessing these two completely different kinds of interventions work synergistically with each other. It is very common for a person to derive greater benefit from psychotherapy after starting a well-prescribed medication. When their brain is working better, they are simply more able to respond. The reverse is also true—a person may only get limited benefit even from a well-prescribed medication until they start working with the kind of therapy that is needed for their situation.

> **The interventions in this book are the third leg of the stool that are so often overlooked in today's medical landscape. They will never substitute for well-prescribed medications or psychotherapy. But they will support each, working synergistically with the other therapies to help people's bodies and brains function optimally.**

There will be times when using this functional, integrative approach will help some people no longer need certain medications. When people start to address the underlying physiological issues that are causing imbalances, they often discover that medications were poor substitutes for addressing the underlying issues. But this does not always happen, and nor is it the point. Many people will continue to need medication, even after addressing all the underlying causes. The true and highest goal of medicine is to help people function at their best, utilizing any and all effective tools in the process.

People benefit the most when practitioners work together to truly understand a patient, and help the patient access all the forms of medicine appropriate for his/her unique situation. In this customized approach, functional medicine provides a methodology to understand the patient, and integrative medicine provides the tools to help the patient.

## CASE STUDY

# Accelerate and Improve Therapeutic Results

The world of psychotherapy includes a large and diverse assortment of powerful techniques, tools, and skills that effectively boost people's ability to cope with life, stress, and relationships. The most exciting part of practicing integrative medicine is witnessing people respond to psychotherapy faster, and with greater depth. When people's brains are working better, their ability to respond to any and all therapy techniques improves. The following case study illustrates how that can happen, sometimes dramatically.

Christopher first came to my office several years ago when he was 10 years old. Both of his parents brought him to his first visit. Christopher had a few different diagnoses over the years, but his parents didn't feel any of them truly matched what the issue was. The core issue was his anger outbursts. When he got frustrated or upset, his temper would explode, and often a two-year-old temper tantrum kind of scene would unfold, with yelling, crying, and physical acting out.

These outbursts had been going on since he was a toddler and could happen at home, school, and often while playing sports. A classic trigger for Christopher was striking out in a baseball game. He loved baseball, and was quite talented at it, but if he struck out, or if someone on his team struck out at a key moment, he didn't just get upset, he could lose control. After these outbursts, he would feel embarrassed and ashamed, and apologize for his behavior.

Before Christopher's parents sought a functional medicine approach, they had seen a few different specialists. Christopher had first been diagnosed with ADHD, but the ADHD medications made his symptoms dramatically worse instead of better. Another doctor had diagnosed it as an anxiety disorder; both Christopher and his parents really felt that the anxiety he felt was a *result* of the issue, not a cause of the issue. He had briefly tried an anti-anxiety medication, but it had no effect. He had been seeing a private therapist for almost three years, and his parents felt it had helped some, but Christopher still struggled more than they hoped he would.

As I talked with Christopher about how and when he experienced his anger and various situations, both stressful and not stressful, it became clear that even when he was calm, he was in a chronically hyper-stimulated state. He was very sensitive to both physical and emotional stimuli, but usually he could control his reaction. When something did make him angry, he said he wasn't really sure what happened, and his parents described his behavior as "losing control."

One of the more common triggers for this kind of hypersensitivity is an inflammatory reaction to synthetic food dyes. When I first asked his parents about how much of these chemicals Christopher consumed, they said, "Almost none." But after they went home and really started looking carefully at all the food in their house, they found it was in far more things than they suspected. It's not just the Skittles, Fruit Loops, and other obvious sources of food coloring that are the problem; these chemicals are lurking in an amazing number of packaged foods. Completely avoiding food colorings requires   diligently checking *every* label, and often people learn to shop somewhat differently.

Once Christopher's parents had a system down, the resulting change was remarkable. They were surprised just how quickly Christopher's symptoms improved. One week after he stopped consuming any food dyes, his parents reported he had 75 percent fewer tantrums.

These dramatic results are not as unusual as people sometimes think. There is a myth that natural therapies "take longer." In fact, they often work very quickly—what *can* take a long time is helping people understand why they need to make changes and motivating them to actually do it. But once the brain gets what it needs, or stops being exposed to a substance that causes an inflammatory reaction, improvement often happens quite rapidly.

When I next saw Christopher for a follow-up, I asked him a lot of questions to try to determine what had changed, what hadn't changed, and just how much it had changed. When I asked him about certain stressful situations, such as the ones he had described earlier playing sports, he replied, "Well, what's most different is that now the tools in my toolbox work."

What a lucid description from a 10-year-old describing his different experiences with all the techniques he had for managing anger and self-soothing! Christopher had successfully learned what he was supposed to do when he got upset, but his previous experience was that those techniques did not work very well. Now that his brain was in a more normal state, he was experiencing waves of emotions, instead of tsunamis of emotions. His techniques seemed to work much more effectively.

This case illustrates how people can need more than one kind of intervention, and not until those interventions are used together does the person really experience a dramatic change. But even therapy and avoiding food colorings were not enough—his parents were right, he was about 75 percent better. It took a couple more months to uncover the other issue that was contributing to Christopher's symptoms. More on this case in Chapter 5.

People needing more than one kind of intervention is not unique to integrative or functional medicine. It is not uncommon for people to start responding better to psychotherapy after being prescribed the right medication. The opposite can also be true—some people will have a better overall response to a medication after starting needed psychotherapy. Treating the nutritional, environmental, and lifestyle factors is the third leg of the stool. No one intervention can substitute for the others when they are needed. While the metaphor is imperfect, because people don't always need all three, the best medicine always involves a thorough examination to determine which interventions are needed, and integrates those that are appropriate.

# Asking the Right Questions: Assessment and Interview

Medical research is a long and involved process of evaluating both efficacy and safety of an intervention. When investigating how a certain chemical compound affects the body, whether it is a natural compound or a synthesized drug, testing starts with investigating how different molecules affect each other, then how the compound affects cells, and then research typically moves into studies on animals. Only after both efficacy and safety have been demonstrated in animal models do clinical trials in humans start.

But all too often, the media reports on an exciting discovery of early medical research, and it gets interpreted as a proven cure. This happens with both conventional therapies as well as natural therapies. Early research can indeed be very exciting when a new possibility is discovered. But every stage of medical research is critically important and needs to be interpreted in the correct context. Without early research, doctors couldn't know what to even test in clinical trials. But without clinical trials, a huge amount of money and hope can be wasted treating people with interventions that at best do not help, and at worst, can be dangerous. All the information in this book is based on clinical research that has completed the full process and has been proven to be effective in trials involving humans.

Even when clinical research exists, interpreting the research can still be controversial. The quality of the study, the size of the study, and the nature of the study all impact how the results should be interpreted. Very rarely do these details get mentioned in the headline reporting the study's conclusion. But without the context those details provide, it is impossible to correctly interpret the conclusion.

> **The biggest hurdle with clinical practice is knowing how to apply all the research: No research study is ever going to tell a practitioner exactly what the person sitting in their office tomorrow at 11 am is going to need. Figuring out which "proven" intervention will help the next person suffering a particular condition is never an easy task. Interpreting and effectively applying the vast amount of information available from clinical research requires practicing the art of medicine.**

For example, there are many drugs and over-the-counter remedies that have significant amounts of research "proving" their effectiveness. But if a practitioner simply tries one remedy after another, hoping one hits the mark, this "shotgun approach" is as likely to harm the patient as it is to help. To truly help the patient, the practitioner needs to know a lot more than just if the remedy has been tested. The practitioner needs to also know *how* the remedy works, *and* whether the remedy addresses the underlying cause of a person's symptoms. **"Proof" that a remedy "works" does not necessarily yield effective medicine.** Knowing which remedies will work in each unique clinical situation requires both a deep understanding of the remedy as well as a deep understanding of the patient. As research grows, the complexity of the process grows. So does the potential to help. When there are more remedies available, it can be harder to know where to start. It all comes back to the deeper analysis of the patient and determining the underlying causes of symptoms referred to in Chapter 1. The rest of the book will explain how to correct the most common causes underlying mental illness.

# Comprehensive Assessment

In a world pressed for time, doctors pressured to see the next patient, patients wanting an immediate answer, and a medical system that over-values tests, the clinical interview often gets short-changed. Seen as time-consuming and subjective, and the subjective seen as unreliable, the clinical visit has been made shorter and shallower. This approach neglects the single most powerful tool available to medical practitioners.

With acute, non-life threatening problems, problem-focused interviews are appropriate. However, mental illness, like all chronic diseases, invariably influences and is influenced by every aspect of a person's physical and social state. Knowing these details is essential to understanding each particular patient. Each patient is unique, and every case of depression, anxiety, bipolar, or ADHD differs somewhat from every other case of the same diagnosis.

A thorough clinical interview will uncover the information necessary to understand the nature of illness, the etiological factors, and any exacerbating conditions and obstacles to change. An interview conducted by a functional medicine doctor attempting to fully elucidate the complete nature of diseases affecting an individual is somewhat more comprehensive than an interview conducted by a mental health practitioner. But since mental and physical health are so intimately related, understanding the process of deeper evaluation can augment the mental health practitioner's ability to recognize common patterns and more effectively guide people toward complete care. **There are two primary goals for this comprehensive assessment:**

1. Dig deeper for organic causes of mental and emotional symptoms.
2. Elucidate patterns of dysfunction from a tangled symptom complex.

### The Interview

Regardless of the length or depth of the interview, the most critical aspect of the interview is establishing a sense of rapport and trust. This connection is built via the tone of the questions as much as the nature of the questions because gaining trust requires not only extensive knowledge but also genuine feelings of interest in and compassion for the patient. The rest of this section is going to detail how to apply biochemical and physiological knowledge to the daily practice of medicine. Essential to this process are the skills of asking open-ended questions, attentive listening and observation, and responding to the patient in a manner that makes them feel safe and understood. This includes not only listening and responding to the patient's verbal answers, but also their body language and emotions at all times. If a patient does not feel comfortable in the interview and safe while talking about difficult topics, no amount of time and questioning will coerce the patient to reveal the personal details necessary for a truly thorough understanding of his/her state. However, responding to a patient's discomfort or pain, either physical or emotional, will lay the foundation for trust. Rapport starts in the first visit, and each subsequent interaction builds it.

The following sections will detail the elements of a comprehensive interview, including specific questions to ask in order to get the most clear and useful information possible. For example, asking someone how they sleep will often yield the answer "fine." However, asking, "Do you wake feeling rested?" will often be answered with a no, which indicates further questioning is needed, despite reporting "fine" sleep.

### The Intake Form

One could argue that the interview really begins with the intake form, because the questions prime the patient for the type and depth of the interview. It also gives the patient a chance to pre-record detailed information that can be overly time-consuming during the interview, such as medication dosages, saving time for both the medical assistant as well as the doctor. A useful intake form also primes the doctor, providing an overview of the scope and nature of the problem as well as previewing issues that will need to be questioned in more detail during the interview.

Most intake forms are completed in the office prior to the first visit. While I am unaware of any data on this, I think it is interesting to note that when I started using an online form, completed at home prior to the first visit, the quality of information I received increased dramatically. (Previously I had used a paper form, which was also completed at home.) As will be illustrated through the rest of this section, asking a combination of both open-ended and targeted questions often leads to the most comprehensive information.

## Present Illness

### Chief Complaint—The Patient's Statement of What the Problem is

The chief complaint is fundamental to understanding the patient's feeling of what is most important, and his/her understanding of the problem. Even if other issues turn out to be more fundamental to starting treatment, it is critical to return to the chief complaint and explain how your treatment plan relates specifically to it.

## Details of Current Symptoms: Nature, Quality, Severity, Timing, Setting, Factors that Affect the Symptoms (Positively and Negatively)

The answers to these questions provide the framework for the rest of the interview because the primary goal is to create a working explanation of how all these factors relate to each other.

### Significant Negatives

When an aspect of common patterns is missing, that is always a red flag to investigate. For instance, most people who are anxious have trouble falling asleep. However if a person states that despite ongoing anxiety and panic attacks, they have no difficulty sleeping, it is unlikely their anxiety is due to some of the hormonal imbalances that cause both anxiety and sleep disturbance.

### History of the Development of Symptoms

The history of onset of symptoms, treatments, and reactions to past treatments will almost always steer the practitioner in the direction of the most important underlying etiologies. Some patients will explain the development of their symptoms in detail, but others will have difficulty remembering or will provide questionably accurate information. When the patient is struggling, a useful question is, "When do you last remember feeling truly great?" Starting there and tracing what they do remember will provide at least some of the critical milestones.

If an adult patient answers that he/she has never felt good, ask specifically if she felt badly in childhood, teenage, and early adulthood years. Sometimes she will realize she did feel much better then, or, she truly has suffered these symptoms her whole life. Certain causes of depression manifest even in childhood, whereas some have their onset later in life, and distinguishing between them is important.

### Other Current Illnesses

This is not a review of systems, but asking the patient for any other symptoms that are currently bothering him/her. For each current illness that he/she recognizes, repeat the process of asking about details of current symptoms, history of development, and past treatment results.

### Patient's Response to the Symptoms, and Impact of the Symptoms on Patient's Life

The effects of the symptoms, and/or the patient's response to symptoms often becomes an exacerbating cause, and understanding these relationships is key to breaking the negative cycle. Recognizing the patient's feelings and addressing them is also key to helping the patient feel listened to and understood, which is necessary for clear communication and trust.

### Patient's Thoughts About, and Interpretation of, Their Own State

Patients sometimes have remarkable insight into their own situation and their own cycle of distress, which can be invaluable to the doctor. Even when his/her impressions are misguided, they are still critical to understanding the patient's full situation, and addressing the patient's concerns.

### Psychiatric Review of Systems

Likely, other issues will have already been identified, but because psychiatric conditions more often than not involve multiple co-morbidities, ask directly if there are other diagnoses, and ask specifically about anxiety, panic, phobias, irritability, moodiness, focus, and addictions.

# Medications

### Medications Currently Taking: A List of Prescriptions, OTC, Vitamins, Herbal Products, and Borrowed Medicines

The list itself is informative, but also ask detailed questions about when the medication was started, what it helps, how much it helps, if they experience any negative effects that they know of, and if they have ever tried stopping the medicine, what was his/her experience? You might be surprised how many people either do not know why they are taking certain things, or claim that it helps something it was never meant to help. All of this data provides clues to which treatments may, or likely won't, be helpful.

### Medications Taken in the Past

This list does not need to be as detailed, because likely the patient won't remember exact details, but responses to past treatments is critical information, and often patients need to be asked about past treatments in different ways to fully complete the timeline. Also, it is a helpful transition into asking about other health history, and starts the process of knowing when and which medical records might be necessary to access to get complete information. Some details, such as past psychiatric prescriptions, need to be known in detail. Other issues, such as antibiotics for upper respiratory infections likely don't need to be quantified exactly, but a general sense of frequency and tolerance can be key information.

# History

### Childhood Illnesses, Adult Illnesses, Hospitalizations, Operations/Procedures, Accidents/Injuries

Any of these factors can be significant etiologies, even if the patient does not recognize the association, so these possibilities need to be asked about specifically. The intake form is a good place to jog patients' memories about past events, but even if nothing is written down, the interview should review these questions.

# Quality of Life

### Energy

"Fatigue" will be a remarkably common complaint, but just like depression, not all fatigue is the same. The specifics of the nature, severity, timing, history, and progression of the fatigue all point to different potential etiologies. Specifically ask when the patient experiences the best and worst energy during the day and month, and if there is an afternoon "lull" or "crash," and if he/she tends to experience a "second wind."

### Sleep

The fundamental questions about sleep are, "Do you wake feeling refreshed?" and, "Is your energy stable and high throughout the day?" If the patient answers no to either of these questions, the doctor needs to question the patient about the details of sleep patterns and habits. Sleep issues may be playing a role in either causing or exacerbating the main issues.

# Lifestyle

### Alcohol

Moderate alcohol consumption does not threaten health, and the detrimental effect of excessive alcohol consumption is well-known. However, many people do not understand what moderate alcohol consumption is, and of course, many people who struggle with alcohol addictions will underestimate or hide the amount of alcohol they consume. Asking direct questions does not always yield the most accurate information.

### Caffeine Intake

Because of its ubiquitous presence, most people, including doctors, tend to forget that caffeine is a drug, and, like all drugs, can have both positive and negative effects. Also like all drugs, the effects vary from person to person and can affect the same person differently after health changes. Carefully quantifying caffeine intake is as important as knowing medication dosages because caffeine so frequently causes or exacerbates hormonal imbalances, insomnia, anxiety, panic attacks, and palpitations, all of which are frequent complaints. Because addressing the issue of caffeine is so critical and commonly overlooked, particularly in regards to mental health, it will be discussed in more detail in Chapter 5.

### Diet

Assessing diet for adequate intake of protein, essential fats, vitamins, minerals, and calories is critical to building the foundation for proper neurotransmitter functioning. The level of detail needed will depend on how close to the edge the patient is. A one-day diet recall on an intake form typically gives a working impression of where someone likely is on the spectrum, though it is important to verify that his/her answer reflects his/her typical habits. If the patient is not regularly consuming protein at least three times per day, including breakfast, as well as several servings of vegetables daily, and nuts and/or high quality fatty fish regularly, then working with diet will need to be part of restoring and maintaining optimal health.

### Exercise/Activity

Assess typical activities and exercise for a week, including occupation. If the patient is not engaged in regular physical activity, the obstacles to regular activity will need to be addressed as part of a complete recovery plan.

### Social

The social environment that an individual lives in affects his/her physical and mental/emotional health. The nature of the environment, as well as the patient's own feelings about their environment are critically important. Specifically asking if the patient feels supported by family and friends, and comparing that with any factual data available is a critical piece of the assessment.

## Review of Systems

The review of systems finishes the interview by specifically asking about topics that can help the doctor understand the pattern and hierarchy of dysfunction. All too often, psychiatrists focus on categorizing the exact nature of the mental/emotional state, overlook physical symptoms, and miss very clear signals about direct organic causes of the chief complaints. The patient also often does not recognize physical symptoms as relevant to mental health complaints, or may simply have overlooked them while discussing the patient's more dramatic or severe symptoms. However, these seemingly superfluous symptoms often contain important clues and reveal or confirm a deeper pattern of dysfunction.

### Allergies

Ask specifically about reactions to drugs, environments, seasons, and foods, including details of what the reaction is, and how predictable it is. Different types of allergies indicate various kinds of immune imbalance and inflammation, which if present, are likely playing a role in the patient's symptoms.

### Weight

Any recent changes and history of any substantial gains or losses can explain how dietary patterns different from the current pattern may have played a role in nutrient deficiencies. It is important to remember that excessive dieting can be as or more detrimental than excessive eating. Hormonal swings can also play a role in weight changes, and may be critical to understanding the current hormonal situation.

### Skin

Any chronic skin issues, or history of them, can provide clues to inflammation, immune imbalance, gut disturbance, hormonal imbalances, and the presence of toxins.

## Headaches

The nature and timing of headaches can indicate allergies, inflammation, hormonal imbalances, nutrient deficiencies, and food reactions.

## Sinuses/Nose/Ears

Chronic problems in these areas can provide further clues to allergies, inflammation, food reactions, and toxin exposures.

## Mouth/Throat

Always include a review of dental health—again, either current or past problems can be part of issues with inflammation, immune imbalance or stress, gastrointestinal problems, food reactions, and toxin exposures.

## Neck/Thyroid

In every case of depression, thyroid issues need to be suspected until ruled out, and detailed questioning about thyroid symptoms as well as a thyroid exam are critical for understanding lab results.

## Respiratory

Chronic respiratory issues can be signs of allergies, digestive disturbance, and inflammation. Also chronic low-grade hypoxia from asthma, chronic obstructive pulmonary disease, or sleep apnea can be direct causes of nearly all mental/emotional issues.

## Cardiac

Cardiac issues can either be evidence of, or causative of, inflammation and mitochondrial dysfunction. They are also always a source of significant stress and sometimes even trauma, and need to be recognized as such.

## Gastrointestinal (GI)

Surprisingly often, people do not even recognize their own digestive symptoms as problems because they have been living with them for so long. Therefore, it is critical to ask specifics about digestion, even when someone reports their digestion is "fine." Always ask about feelings of discomfort or bloating, feeling like clothes fit differently in the evening from in the morning, frequency and ease of bowel movements, heartburn, indigestion, and ask again about taking over-the-counter meds in the context of digestion. The presence of any of these symptoms indicates imbalance in the gut, which is key to the gut-brain connection, as well as potential issues with inflammation, allergies, and nutrient deficiency.

## Genitourinary

Because hormones play such a huge role in depression, always ask female patients about the nature of their menstrual cycle, including regularity, length and amount of bleeding, any pain/

discomfort/cramping, and pre-menstrual symptoms. How the woman felt during and after any pregnancies can also provide strong clues to both past and current hormone imbalances. In menopausal/peri-menopausal women, ask about related symptoms, present and past, both physical and emotional.

Male patients should be screened for symptoms of erectile dysfunction and benign prostatic hypertrophy, as both can be symptoms of hormone imbalances and excess inflammation.

### Musculoskeletal

Patients often do not recognize the impact of pain on other aspects of health, or they learn to live with it by ignoring it, so it is important to ask specifically about pain. It can often be difficult to tease out the multi-faceted relationships between mental health symptoms and various pain syndromes.

### Neuro

Neurological symptoms can be signs of nutrient deficiency, inflammation, and allergies. Even mild or intermittent symptoms of numbness/tingling, tremors, restless legs, or pain can be important signs. The presence of diagnosable neurological symptoms is always significant.

## Family History

The family history provides a crucial context to evaluate a patient's condition. Simply asking if family members had diagnoses of depression and other mental illness is not sufficient because mental illness is not always recognized as such, particularly in older generations. Ask specifically about behaviors that can reflect mental illness: suicides, addictions, hospitalizations, incarcerations, and withdrawal from family or society. Include three generations: siblings, cousins, parents, aunts, uncles, and grandparents.

## Other Professional Opinions

Are there other professionals already involved in the case? Was there a referral? Are there other social services involved in the case? Reports from all of these connections should be gathered if present. After you have had a chance to review them, do others' impressions correlate or differ significantly from your own? Are there any professional opinions that are conspicuously missing? Regardless of the answer, it is a critical aspect to the case.

Also, what is the patient's view of these relationships? The answers to all of these questions are important for interpreting the reliability and accuracy of the patient's description of their own condition, as well as communicating effectively with the patient.

## Organizing Symptoms into Diagnosis

Throughout the interview, as the patient's symptoms are being examined, the doctor will develop and explore numerous hypotheses about how all of the factors discussed up to this point do, or do not, underlie this particular patient's symptoms. As these hypotheses emerge, targeted questioning will seek and reveal additional evidence that verifies or contradicts those hypotheses. Other hypotheses require laboratory testing to verify or quantify certain etiologies. All these patterns eventually need to be organized into a functional diagnosis and then synthesized into a treatment plan. The next chapter will detail that process.

# Breaking the
# Vicious Cycles of Disease

## Organic Causes of Mental Illness

The DSM-5 states repeatedly, as a caveat of nearly every diagnosis, that "organic causes of the symptoms have been ruled out." Typically, an intake does screen for drug reactions as well as other diagnoses that are known causes of depression. But all too often, doctors do not check for other physical causes of depression such as nutrient deficiency, hormonal imbalances, and inflammatory responses. Instead, doctors jump to the conclusion of neurotransmitter imbalance that is somehow independent of the rest of physiology. Neurotransmitter imbalances are very common, and sometimes may be genetic or due to factors completely beyond our control. However, a careful analysis of all the factors that can disrupt neurotransmitters is necessary before determining that a Prozac deficiency is causing the depression.

## Distinguishing Patterns of Dysfunction
## From a Tangled Symptom Complex

Even after determining that a person's symptoms fit into a box labeled "depression," "ADHD," or any other disease or even any of the many sub-types of the different major categories of diagnosis, the doctor still needs to understand how each patient's unique combination of symptoms and causative factors influence each other. Without that level of understanding, any attempts to alter the pattern will simply be blind guesses. Differential diagnosis demonstrates that any particular symptom almost always has more than one possible cause and that the same disease-causing problem will manifest somewhat differently in different individuals.

Simply asking for every possible symptom and etiology only yields a longer list of symptoms. The key question through the entire process of interviewing and analyzing is, "How do these symptoms relate to other symptoms?" Even after one diagnosis is clear—keep asking how all the diagnoses and symptoms fit together. A truly effective interview done by a knowledgeable practitioner traces combinations of symptoms back to root etiologies, usually revealing a positive feedback loop.

In chronic disease, there is almost always a positive feedback cycle, where one issue causes another issue, and in turn the second issue causes the first. There are usually more than two steps in the cycle, and often multiple cycles contributing to the problem. These self-perpetuating cycles cause disease to become chronic, and breaking them is the only way to heal chronic disease. **Recognizing these positive feedback loops within the tangled symptom complex is the goal of the interview and the foundation of functional diagnosis.**

Positive feedback loops tend to grow more complicated over time, as new layers of symptoms, responses, and etiologies develop, sometimes masking or confusing the fundamental issue. If someone is eating a very poor diet, it may appear that it is causing depression as well as gastrointestinal malfunction. While eating a more nutritious diet will be part of long-term healing for that patient, you will not help the patient if you simply recommend dietary change without understanding that it was gastrointestinal distress that first caused the patient to stop eating certain foods. Further complicating the issue might be medications prescribed for the gastrointestinal symptoms, which exacerbated the nutrient deficiency. In this case, treating depression means first healing the gut, removing the need for medication, and then restoring nutrient intake through diet and possibly supplementation.

The DSM-5 offers many different categories that describe variations on the symptoms of various disease, but it does not categorize diagnoses in terms of what physiological factors are playing a role. It is well accepted, though arguable, that neurotransmitter imbalances are the physiological basis of many mental health issues, and the goal of a functional diagnosis is to understand the causes of the neurotransmitter imbalance. This process is deeper and more complex than simply ruling out other medical conditions as the cause of the depression. Rather, it is examining the patient holistically, based on the premise that both physical and psychological factors influence the neurotransmitters that regulate mood.

> The goal of functional diagnosis is to understand how the symptoms and responses fit together, creating positive feedback cycles, and how those cycles relate to each other. That level of functional diagnosis will point toward where and how to break the cycles, and help the patient move toward health.

The positive feedback cycles arise from both physical and psychological factors. Some factors are the symptoms themselves, and some are the patient's response to the symptoms. A very simple example of a feedback loop is:

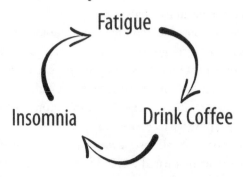

Fatigue

Insomnia

Drink Coffee

The obvious answer in the previous case is to stop drinking coffee. If there are no other factors involved, that treatment will solve both the insomnia and the fatigue. While this problem is extremely common, rarely is it that simple. There are usually other factors affecting multiple aspects of the cycle. If something else is also causing the fatigue, stopping the coffee may help the sleep, but the patient still does not feel better, and may feel worse. Digging a little deeper may reveal:

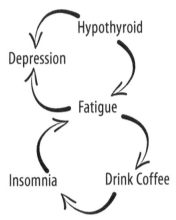

Now there is a new obvious answer: treat the thyroid. In simple cases, this will correct the problem. But sometimes the clearly indicated treatment does not yield the expected result, and instead uncovers another set of factors that need to be understood. In this case, instead of feeling better on thyroid treatment, the patient experienced palpitations, even more trouble sleeping, and anxiety:

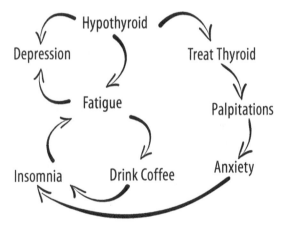

This example illustrates how the whole picture does not always reveal itself at once, even with appropriate testing and treatment. Only after the unexpected response to thyroid medication did the picture of adrenal imbalance emerge. If adrenal testing had been done along with the thyroid testing, it would have been impossible to interpret the results until after treating the thyroid. Quite possibly, this same patient could have shown low adrenal function on testing, but still tolerated the thyroid treatment and shown improvement in both fatigue and depression. In that case, adrenal recovery would have happened spontaneously  after the thyroid was corrected, without any further intervention. Giving adrenal support when it is not needed can overstimulate the patient and interfere with healing. This example demonstrates that **the most important test is how the patient responds, and that trying to do too much at once can be as problematic as not digging deep enough.**

Most likely, this scenario all happened years before the patient sought integrative care. During the following years, the thyroid dose has been adjusted to eliminate the palpitations and she has been put on an SSRI for the depression, a stimulant medication for the poor focus and fatigue, and a sedative to help with sleep. She finally seeks integrative care because the depression is worsening and she has been switched to a different SSRI twice but she does not feel they help.

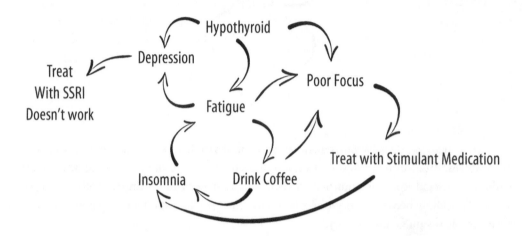

This case illustrates why it is so important to trace the cause and effect of each symptom and intervention until a feedback loop has been established, a functional diagnosis is determined, and treatment is given based on that deeper understanding. The symptomatic treatment she had for years never addressed the underlying issue, and therefore had limited effectiveness. The SSRI never fully worked and lost its effectiveness with time because it did not address the underlying cause of the low serotonin. As her body adapted to the SSRI, she returned to the state of low serotonin and depression that the hormonal imbalance was causing all along. The stimulant and sedative medications addressed symptoms, providing temporary symptom relief, but in doing so also fed parts of the cycle, making the overall problem worse instead of better.

The functional diagnosis offers a whole new range of treatment options. By looking at the patterns of symptoms, rather than just a collection of symptoms, another diagnosis emerges—adrenal imbalance. Addressing that issue helps several of the symptoms directly: depression, anxiety, fatigue, insomnia. It also allows the patient to tolerate full treatment of the hypothyroidism, further helping the depression, anxiety, and fatigue. As the patient starts to feel better, she is more capable of engaging in important therapies such as psychotherapy and exercise, and these therapies start benefiting her dramatically more.

Understanding the larger patterns of dysfunction are equally important even with interventions that are simply healthy habits. Educating a patient about healthy habits may be necessary, but unless the entire problem is the patient's ignorance of what healthy habits are, that alone will not help. The vast majority of patients have multiple obstacles to changing habits, and without addressing those obstacles to change, change is unlikely to happen. In this case, a superficial analysis does reveal that poor sleep is causing fatigue, poor focus, and depression. However, simply working with sleep habits or using alternative therapies to sleep medication will not be effective because they do not address the underlying hormonal and neurochemical imbalances that are disrupting sleep any more than sedative medications do.

The integrative nature of functional diagnosis requires an equally integrative approach to treatment plans. Patterns of dysfunction overlap, but each patient is unique, and therefore needs a personalized treatment plan that accounts for individual variation. There is not one protocol that works for everyone, or even everyone with a given diagnosis. Even similar patterns of dysfunction can require different combinations of treatments, and often substantially different dosing. But the foundation necessary to translate all the various symptom complexes into a hierarchal treatment plan is understanding the functional diagnosis.

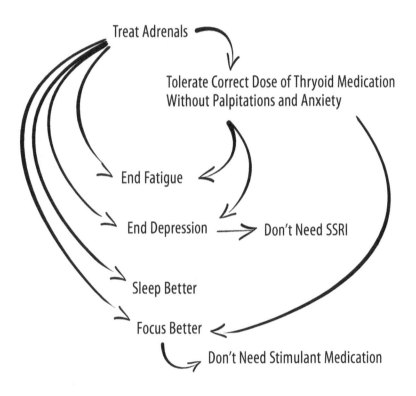

# The Mental Health Clinician's Role in Integrative Medicine: Scope of Practice Issues

Not every mental health practitioner is licensed to diagnose and prescribe treatments. Because there is such a wide range of degrees and skill sets, it is impossible to give any definitive recommendations that apply to everyone. Every professional needs to be aware of the limits of their scope of practice as well as their own knowledge and abilities. And every professional needs to be aware of the resources and therapies available outside of their own skill set. Sometimes the best way to serve a patient is to help them access the care they need, even if it's not something you can offer personally.

Without training specifically in functional medicine, making a complete functional medicine diagnosis will be outside the scope of practice. The last chapter certainly does not provide that level of training, but it introduces the kind of thinking necessary, *and available*, to solve complex cases. Complex cases always require more than one intervention, and knowing when and where to refer for other kinds of help is a critical aspect of helping patients for *all* professionals. Because functional medicine is not currently easily accessible within the conventional medical system, it is that much more important to help the people who need it most access it.

Sometimes practitioners ask, "But how do I convince someone to look at all these issues when they can just take drugs instead?" Very simply, you don't. If someone is getting a positive and desired response from a medication or medications, consider that person lucky. But most practitioners see many people who have tried multiple medications, and despite those medications are still suffering significant symptoms. When people are looking for answers and not finding solutions, educating them about the issues that have not been addressed in their health, and helping them find the help they need is paramount.

Within the scope of practice for every mental health professional is education. Patients need education not just to help them understand their condition, but also to understand all the different factors that contribute to both health and disease. Working with people on the environmental and lifestyle issues that are so critical to maintaining health is all too often overlooked by today's medical system. Working with people on these fundamental issues is sometimes the key piece that is missing and preventing other therapies from working. When these underlying issues finally get addressed, other necessary therapies actually start working better.

For example, many people struggle terribly with getting adequate sleep, despite taking sleep medications. If the person does not feel safe in their environment, the brain cannot relax and fall asleep because to do so would be to risk injury. Even if a sedative sleep medication is introduced, the body will fight against it simply because it is trying to survive. Only after the issue of safety is addressed, can the sleep medication work. But the doctor who prescribes the sleep medication very rarely has the skills necessary to address the safety issue, while the mental health practitioner who is trained to help the person address the physical environment, psychological issues, and relationship issues may not be licensed to prescribe sleep medication. This example shows why integrative care is so critical.

Countless more examples arise when the issues of nutrition start to be addressed. Nutrition is a large and complex subject, ranging from the basics of healthy eating, to treating specific nutrient deficiencies, to recommending specialized diets because of the impact of certain diseases. The information in this book will not make you an expert in nutrition, sleep, or physiology, but it will teach you the basics necessary to work with the fundamentals that support optimal brain function and mental health.

**Never underestimate how powerful these fundamentals are.** So often they are the underlying causes behind a person's symptoms. Even when the problem didn't start because of issues with sleep or nutrition, mental health issues often negatively impact lifestyle and ability for self-care, and then those issues aggravate the underlying disease. People with ADHD or bipolar almost always have sleep issues. When all aspects of those sleep issues are not addressed, and instead the medication gets changed, the real issue has not been addressed.

Never underestimate how powerful it can be to work with the fundamentals! So much of helping people with these lifestyle factors involves helping people overcome obstacles to change. Education is usually just the very beginning. Think of how many patients are going to get told by their doctor, "Your health condition would improve significantly if you lose weight." How many of those patients are going to immediately know exactly what they have to do, and do it? The process of losing weight, of making any lifestyle change, is a much deeper psychological process than simply knowing what the goal is. Most people need help with that process. This is where the mental health practitioner's skills are invaluable. Quite simply, you don't need a degree in nutrition to educate people about the importance and value of eating a balanced breakfast. But you may well need a degree in counseling to get someone to actually start eating breakfast.

# The Physical Basis of Mental Health

## Sleep, Activity, and Food

SECTION 2

*Compromising any of these three foundations — sleep, activity and food — always compromises brain function, yet modern medicine typically overlooks thoroughly addressing these issues.*

These three foundations of health are all equally critical to the brain function necessary for stable, appropriate mood and optimum mental clarity. No one of them can substitute for any of the others. Eating an excellent diet can never make up for inadequate sleep. Plenty of sleep will never compensate for inadequate activity.

**Nor can any medication or drug ever fully rectify the damage caused by poor sleep, activity, or food.** Not only do drugs used in this way not help, sometimes they actually make the problem worse. For example, feeling tired from inadequate sleep causes difficulty focusing and diminishes executive functioning. A stimulant medication can help with those issues, but it can also disrupt sleep. Additional sleep disruption further exacerbates the symptoms, increasing the need for the medication, without fixing the underlying problem. Both pharmaceutical prescriptions as well as non-prescription drugs can be implicated.

# Helping Your Client Get Adequate Sleep

The importance of addressing sleep issues when working with mental health issues simply cannot be overstated. When the human brain does not get adequate quality sleep, it leads to feelings of depression, anxiety, moodiness, and diminished executive functioning. If the sleep issues continue long enough or get severe enough, it is only a matter of time until the symptoms result in a diagnosis of a mood disorder, ADHD, or even psychosis.

Inadequate sleep is a very common underlying cause of these symptoms. But many of these disorders (anxiety, ADHD, bipolar) also cause sleep disruption. With ADHD, even the treatments can further disrupt sleep patterns. Lack of sleep then intensifies the symptoms of disease, which further disrupts sleep, and the person becomes trapped in a vicious cycle of disease as described in Chapter 3.

When someone is stuck deep in this cycle (and many people are), it can sometimes seem that both their sleep issues and symptoms are intractable. Breaking out of this cycle and helping the person heal requires treating sleep issues in multiple ways. There are many obstacles to refreshing sleep, some physiological, some environmental, some lifestyle-related, and many that are all three. But to establish healthy sleep patterns, all of these issues need to be addressed.

The more entrenched and long-term the sleep issues are, the more important it is to go back to address the fundamentals necessary for refreshing sleep. **All too often, the conventional medical world only addresses these issues with medication, without addressing the basic fundamentals necessary for healthy, restorative sleep.** Medication will play a necessary role in many cases, but it can never substitute for the fundamentals. You may be the first person who addresses these fundamentals and helps the person overcome their obstacles to healthy sleep patterns.

## How Much Sleep is Enough?

Getting "adequate" sleep first begs the question, "How much is enough sleep?" Many people do not realize how much sleep they require to function at their best, and they may not even realize that they are under-sleeping. Almost everyone has heard the widely publicized advice: "Humans need eight hours of sleep." Even though most lay people have heard it, too, modern life values "doing" and often undervalues relaxation and sleep. Many people convince themselves they do not actually need eight hours, for a variety of reasons. Particularly when people get stressed, sleep is likely to be shortchanged. Very rarely do people go to the doctor and say, "I just don't have enough time to sleep, I need help with time and priority management." They may not even complain of feeling tired. Much more likely they will complain of feeling unmotivated, moody, down, anxious, and/or struggling with focus and productivity.

Even if the doctor asks about sleep, many people will say, "I sleep fine." Unless the doctor asks more detailed questions about their sleep patterns, the fact that the person's symptoms are being caused by inadequate sleep will go overlooked. Even if the doctor does ask, some people need more than the eight hours that is typically recommended as adequate sleep. Eight hours is the average among humans; it represents the top of the bell curve. Many people will function at their best with approximately eight hours of sleep, but some people do need more, and some people can thrive with somewhat less.

Therefore, making a one-size-fits-all recommendation about sleep is not helpful. The real goal is to help people learn what their individual sleep needs are, how to meet those needs, and experience how much better they feel with adequate sleep. **Two critical questions help determine if someone is getting enough sleep:**

1. Do you wake feeling refreshed?
2. Do you have high energy and good mood throughout the whole day?

When someone answers yes to both of those questions, chances are they are getting enough sleep and quality sleep. But when people answer no to either (or both) of those questions, more investigation is needed. Sometimes people answer yes, but later realize, "I often feel sleepy after lunch" or "Well, I'm kind of grumpy and useless in the morning until I get my coffee." These types of responses indicate that the person likely could benefit from more sleep or better quality sleep.

Making time for adequate sleep often really challenges people. Our current culture values doing rather than relaxing, and when people get busy and stressed with various aspects of job and family, often sleep time is what gets shortchanged. Because these other priorities are important, the process of helping people understand the importance of sleep and making the necessary life changes can require some deep work.

Another common challenge is when people live with a person who seems to need less sleep than they do. If someone's family members or spouse thinks people should only sleep six or seven hours, the person who needs eight or nine hours can feel like they are being lazy or somehow shirking their responsibilities by spending that much time in bed. In this instance, working with people around permission to sleep, both from themselves as well as from their social network, is critically important.

## Disrupted Sleep

For many people, getting adequate sleep is much harder than just spending enough time in bed. They are fully aware that poor sleep is affecting their health, and feel stressed about it, simply adding to the problem. Many people struggle with not being able to fall asleep, or waking up in the middle of the night and staying awake for hours. Other people sleep restlessly, waking often and never getting quality deep sleep. These issues require looking at other factors necessary for refreshing sleep.

If someone has trouble falling asleep, the first thing to examine is their pre-bedtime activities. People need a period of relaxation for the brain to prepare for sleep. Most people cannot go from full activity level to sleeping in just five to 10 minutes; a longer period of relaxation is required. Even though most people can point out someone they know who can fall asleep within minutes of their head hitting the pillow, it is more likely to be a sign of being over-tired than health.

It's also possible that the person was in fact relaxing before bed, but not in a way that is immediately obvious to those around them. What is relaxing to one person may be stimulating to someone else. There is no one perfect way to relax that works for all people. Using phones or other devices with screens before bed can be overstimulating for some people, but other people might use those same devices in a way that induces relaxation and helps them fall asleep. Some research shows that the blue light emitted by these devices can disrupt sleep cycles, but not everyone has the same level of sensitivity.

Even something necessary and beneficial, like exercise, can have different effects on different people. Some people like to exercise in the evening because it helps dissipate excess energy and helps them relax for sleep. Other people find exercise stimulating and have *more* trouble sleeping if they exercise in the evening. These people need to exercise earlier in the day to get the full benefit from exercise.

Some people can do pre-sleep relaxation after they are already in bed. Whether it is reading, listening to music, a meditation, or simply enjoying lying down and slowing down, a significant portion of their bedtime relaxation routine happens in bed. Other people get anxious if they are in bed but not sleeping, so this strategy will not work for them. They need to engage in active relaxation *before* going to bed, so that by the time they are in bed, the brain is prepared for sleep and their anxiety response does not have time to kick in. A back-up plan for what to do if the person finds himself awake 20 minutes later is also helpful in these situations.

Again, the real goal is not to make a one-size-fits-all prescription but to help people figure out an effective relaxation routine. Sometimes the answer can be surprising. One patient who had tried many different yoga routines and styles of meditation finally discovered that she fell asleep most quickly when she cleaned the kitchen before bed. While cleaning the kitchen may not sound like a relaxing activity, it helped her "clean up today and feel prepared for tomorrow," which is in fact a more relaxed state of mind.

> **The bottom line is, if what someone is doing works, don't change it. But if it is not working, even if it "should," help people experiment with new bedtime routines to help them relax.**

Another essential to refreshing sleep that is too often ignored is sleep environment. If the environment is not conducive to sleep, no amount of relaxation before bed is going to be enough. Does the person feel safe in their environment? If a person does not feel safe, it is physiologically impossible to relax. Addressing safety issues can be complex and difficult, but it is critical not only to sleep but to all aspects of health. If there are present physical dangers, that is the absolute first priority to address in any way that it needs to be addressed. If the present situation is safe but there is post-traumatic stress disorder (PTSD), or any kind of emotional residue from past situations, it needs to be dealt with in a totally different way. Using a sleeping medication to try to induce sleep in either situation can actually make sleep problems worse because the body's stress response then fights against the sedative effects. There are no easy answers to treating PTSD, but that's also a critical point—thinking that a sleep medication will be the answer is a false hope that actually exacerbates the problem.

Even in a safe environment, there can be many other issues that disrupt sleep. Noise pollution and light pollution both need to be addressed if present. Interruptions from family or pets can also pose a huge challenge. Quite often, treating sleep issues requires treating a whole family dynamic. Occasional interruptions are an inevitable part of life, but patterns of disruptions that happen every day, like being awakened by pets every morning at 4 am, need to be addressed. You may be the first person who addresses these issues that so often make people feel overwhelmed and helpless.

## Caffeine: Is it Helping or Harming?

The most frequently ignored sleep disrupter is America's drug of choice: caffeine. Caffeine is so ubiquitous in current society that people often forget or don't even realize that it is a drug. Like all drugs, caffeine can be either negative or positive depending on the situation. The positive effects of caffeine include increased alertness and improved focus. These effects are temporary, and often happen without any negative effects. But just as frequently, these positive effects take on the form of a "high" followed by a "low": after the positive effects, the person crashes, leaving them feeling worse than before the positive effect and needing another "hit" to boost them.

Caffeine affects people differently. Some people have a very strong response, some people barely notice it. Some people experience the improved energy from caffeine without any negative effects. But many other people also experience anxiety, sleep disturbance, and heart palpitations. Many people who are suffering negative effects of caffeine do not realize it, mostly because of four persistent myths.

---

### Debunking Caffeine Myths

MYTH 1: I've been drinking coffee for many years, and the sleep problems just started last year, so it can't be that.

TRUTH:

A person's response to caffeine (and all drugs) can change. It changes with age, stress, and other changes in health. While it may be true that the person has used caffeine for years with no negative effects, **if the person currently suffers from**

---

**sleep problems, anxiety, or heart palpitations, the role caffeine is playing *must* be investigated.** Menopause often makes women much more sensitive to the negative effects of caffeine. But it's not just women; men get more sensitive to caffeine with age as well. But it's not just middle-aged or older people—teenagers are also vulnerable to the negative effects of caffeine. When younger people and teenagers are blaming anxiety and sleep issues on high pressure school or job situations, *always* ask about caffeine use. More often it is their response to stress (consuming more caffeine) as much as the stress itself creating problems.

MYTH 2: *I don't have caffeine after noon, so that can't be the reason for my sleep problems.*

TRUTH:

If a person is having trouble falling asleep, consider the evening caffeine first. Stopping caffeine after noon is not enough for some people because **even one cup of coffee or tea at 7am can impact sleep for the next few nights.**

MYTH 3: *I don't have any problem falling asleep; my problem is I wake up in the middle of the night, so it can't be caffeine.*

TRUTH:

Caffeine is typically metabolized out of the body within several hours, but the secondary effects of caffeine on hormones and circadian rhythms can last much longer and can disrupt sleep for days. If someone is having trouble falling asleep, look at the evening or afternoon caffeine first. But if someone is having trouble staying asleep, they wake up in the middle of the night and have trouble falling back asleep, or toss and turn sleeping restlessly, then the morning caffeine is more likely to blame.

MYTH 4: *I only have one cup of coffee; that's not enough to be a problem.*

TRUTH:

Caffeine stimulates the adrenal gland, which partially regulates circadian rhythm. For some people, their body returns to normal after the caffeine "buzz." But for other people, the high is followed by a low, and then this hormonal pendulum keeps swinging, causing people to wake up in the middle of the night.

**The amount of caffeine matters less than *sensitivity* to caffeine.** Because people have such drastically different sensitivities to caffeine, what seems like a lot to one person seems like hardly any to another. As always, the point is to help people understand not just their primary response to caffeine, but also their secondary response.

## How to Determine Response to Caffeine

Many people balk at the thought of going without caffeine. Just about everyone who has ever used caffeine has experienced a time when they either consciously or accidentally skipped their daily dose of caffeine, and they all too vividly remember feeling lethargic, spacey, moody, or worse, and probably the dreaded caffeine withdrawal headache. But all those symptoms are exactly that: withdrawal. Withdrawal symptoms are temporary, and for caffeine, only last a few days. On the third or fourth day of no caffeine, the withdrawal symptoms fade, and over the next few days, the person feels better and better. After one week, most people say, "I feel better without caffeine than I did on caffeine." Their energy is both better and more stable, and their mood both improves and is more stable.

One week is pretty quick to experience more stable energy and mood. Not feeling sleepy in the afternoon helps mood, focus, and productivity. Feeling calmer facilitates better stress management. As sleep improves, and people make up for lost sleep, eventually they start waking up feeling refreshed again. (How long it takes before someone starts feeling truly refreshed depends on how long and how severe the sleep deprivation has been.)

For the fastest results possible, simply eliminate all forms of caffeine, including coffee, tea, soda, energy drinks, and pills. Whether people reduce caffeine slowly or quickly, typically people don't experience any negative effects, or any positive benefits, until they get all the way to no caffeine. If people prefer to go more slowly, that is an option, and can feel more manageable, but it rarely spares the withdrawal effects. Sometimes people think that because reducing caffeine is often easier than they expected, but doesn't improve their symptoms, that full elimination is not necessary. Make sure people understand that they need to fully eliminate caffeine to really know what role caffeine is playing in their symptoms. On the other hand, if people do get full resolution of symptoms with only partial caffeine reduction, then there is no need for them to go further, though that response is unusual.

Decaffeinated varieties of favorite drinks are acceptable alternatives. While decaf coffee and teas do contain tiny amounts of caffeine, it is not usually enough to trigger a reaction in most people. For people who truly love their coffee or tea, decaffeinated varieties are fantastic ways to enjoy the taste and ritual while removing the negative effects. There are rare exceptions—it is possible for some people to be so sensitive to caffeine that even the amount in decaffeinated coffee or tea (or chocolate) can cause a reaction, but switching to decaf will work for the vast majority of people.

If, after a week of avoiding caffeine, withdrawal symptoms still persist, it indicates more needs to be done to support adrenal function (see Chapter 10.) In this case, temporarily going back to using small amounts of caffeine while initiating other support strategies is recommended. Also see Chapter 10 on B-complex as B-vitamin deficiency is one of the primary reasons people suffer extended caffeine withdrawal symptoms.

# The Truth about Caffeine and Sleep

The most frequently ignored sleep disrupter is caffeine. Some people don't experience any negative effects from caffeine, but many others are deeply affected by it.

*Myth 1:* *I've been drinking coffee for many years, and the sleep problems just started last year, so it can't be that.*

**Truth:** A person's response to caffeine (and all drugs) can change. It changes with age, stress, and other changes in health. While it may be true that the person has used caffeine for years with no negative effects, **if you currently suffer from sleep problems, anxiety, or heart palpitations, the role caffeine is playing must be investigated.**

Menopause often makes women much more sensitive to the negative effects of caffeine. But it's not just women; men get more sensitive to caffeine with age as well. But it's not just middle-aged or older people—teenagers are also vulnerable to the negative effects of caffeine. When younger people and teenagers are blaming anxiety and sleep issues on high-pressure school or job situations, *the caffeine may be the real culprit, not the stress.*

*Myth 2:* *I don't have caffeine after noon, so that can't be the reason for my sleep problems.*

**Truth:** If a person is having trouble falling asleep, consider the evening caffeine first. Stopping caffeine after noon is not enough for some people because **even one cup of coffee or tea at 7 am can impact sleep for the next few nights.**

*Myth 3:* *I don't have any problem falling asleep; my problem is I wake up in the middle of the night, so it can't be caffeine.*

**Truth:** Caffeine is typically metabolized out of the body within several hours, but the secondary effects of caffeine on hormones and circadian rhythms can last much longer and can disrupt sleep for days. If you are having trouble falling asleep, look at the evening or afternoon caffeine first. But if you are having trouble staying asleep, or are sleeping restlessly, then the morning caffeine is more likely to blame.

*Myth 4: I only have one cup of coffee; that's not enough to be a problem.*

**Truth:** Caffeine stimulates the adrenal gland, which partially regulates circadian rhythm. For some people, their body returns to normal after the caffeine "buzz." But for other people, the high is followed by a low, and then this hormonal pendulum keeps swinging, causing people to wake up in the middle of the night. **The amount of caffeine matters less than *sensitivity* to caffeine.** Because people have such drastically different sensitivities to caffeine, what seems like a lot to one person seems like hardly any to another.

**How to determine if caffeine is harming you:**

1. Eliminate all caffeine (coffee, tea, soda, energy drinks, and pills) for two weeks.

2. You may experience temporary withdrawal symptoms: lethargy, mood swings, and headache. Those symptoms will pass after a few days.

3. Within one week, most people say, "I feel better now without caffeine than I did on it!"

4. If you still suffer symptoms after one week, you need additional adrenal support. Restart caffeine at half of your usual intake, and contact one of the following resources for a comprehensive evaluation and customized treatment plan.

**Resources**
If you want more support eliminating caffeine for better sleep, visit the below websites and consider working with a doctor of functional medicine or a naturopathic doctor.

www.thirdstonehealth.com
www.functionalmedicine.org
www.naturopathic.org

# Melatonin: How to Use it Safely and Effectively

Melatonin is now widely available and being used more and more as a "natural" sleep aid. Taking melatonin can be a powerful tool to help restore healthy circadian rhythm; however, misunderstandings abound about how and when to use it, lead many people to using it incorrectly.

The human circadian rhythm is regulated primarily by two hormones: melatonin and cortisol. Melatonin increases in the evening, inducing relaxation and sleepiness, while cortisol decreases, effectively diminishing alertness. In the morning, the opposite occurs: melatonin decreases while cortisol rises, stimulating alertness.

When the circadian rhythm has been disrupted, taking melatonin temporarily can help reset the system. Think of jet lag, an acute disruption of circadian rhythm, when it is necessary to adapt to a different cycle literally overnight. Some people adjust quite easily, other people suffer significant jet lag. Taking melatonin for a few days can help the body adjust more quickly, and then the melatonin is no longer needed.

When there is a longer-term disruption to circadian rhythm, melatonin can be similarly helpful. If the sleep disruption has lasted for months or even years, melatonin will be required for more than a few days—in those cases it will take several weeks or a few months. But the point is to still use it short-term, relative to the situation, and then wean off it to restore the body's ability to regulate circadian rhythm on its own. The process can be thought of as jump-starting a car—once the car is working again, there is no need to keep jump-starting it. But if a person continues to need melatonin, it is critical to ask, "Why?" If a person continues to need melatonin long-term, it is like needing to jump-start the car every morning without ever looking at what else needs to be fixed.

## CASE STUDY
# Follow-up on Christopher

Christopher is the 10-year-old described in Chapter 1 with anger outbursts and tantrums. Removing the food dyes and food colorings from his diet dramatically changed his symptoms quickly, but there was still room for improvement. We tried a couple of other dietary interventions, but without any success. Then he improved, seemingly spontaneously, when summer came.

The first thing his therapist, his parents, and I thought was, "What is going on at school that may be a greater stress than any of us appreciated?" We analyzed everything, including all the things in life that changed during summer. One of the things his mother stated was that in the morning, she now let him sleep until he woke up, which was typically about 8 am. During the school year she woke him up at 6 am so he could be ready to get on the school bus at 7 am.

I had asked Christopher and his parents about sleep at the first visit, and no issues had been reported. So I asked Christopher how long it took him to fall asleep. He said it took "forever." When I asked him what he did, he reluctantly admitted that he read or built things with Legos. His parents expressed surprise at this, and so I had them start watching. The kids' bedtime was between 8 and 8:30 pm, and because his parents got up at 5 am most mornings, they went to bed shortly after. When they re-arranged their schedule some, they discovered that Christopher was indeed still awake between 10 and 10:30 pm most nights. He was well-behaved and quiet at those times and stayed in his room, so his parents hadn't realized he wasn't sleeping. At this point, I started to suspect the other cause of Christopher's emotional volatility was simply not getting enough sleep.

During the summer, we simply let him keep his current pattern. But when school started, I had his parents start watching again. The hope was that when he had to get up earlier, he would start falling asleep earlier. But that did not happen—he continued to be awake at 10 pm, and a few weeks into school, the behavior issues started to return. At this point, we were all quite sure that Christopher needed more sleep.

The ideal solution would be to change the school schedule, but that was not possible (as it's not for most kids.) We decided to use melatonin to try to adjust his sleep schedule earlier. We started with 0.5mg of melatonin at about 7:30 pm, and it worked; Christopher was asleep by 9 pm, and more importantly, his behavior returned to normal. We kept him on the melatonin for about three weeks, long enough to be sure that the improvement was not just coincidence, and then weaned him off the melatonin. As much I would love to say everyone lived happily ever after from this point, that's not what happened.

After Christopher was weaned off the melatonin, his difficulty falling asleep returned. This wasn't as much of a surprise as it may sound—melatonin is better at restoring the circadian rhythm to normal than re-setting where normal is. People do have variations in circadian rhythms—some people are early birds, some are night owls, and some are neither; they can adapt to whatever schedule they need to adapt to. Sleeping 10 pm to 8 am is fairly typical for a 10-year-old; in fact, there is research that shows that a significant portion of kids and adolescents function better on more of a night owl time schedule. (If someone, of any age, says they can't fall asleep before 4 am or can't get up before noon that is *not* a night owl schedule. That is a disrupted circadian rhythm.)

The compromise in this case was to put him back on the melatonin for the school year because everyone involved agreed that the benefits of adequate sleep to his health, social/family life, and academics were the primary concern. However, I continued to work with him on some adrenal support to improve his body's ability to adapt to his environment, including an earlier sleep schedule. With time, as his health continued to improve, primarily because he was no longer eating chemicals that put his body in a state of elevated inflammation and stress, he no longer needed the melatonin by the following school year.

# Sleep Problems Action Plan

*Always start by assessing the sleep environment.*

1. Does the person feel safe?
   - Work with all relevant aspects of that issue: physical, emotional, social and environmental. Address PTSD issues if needed.
2. Are people, animals, electronics, noises, or light interrupting sleep?
   - Help people overcome obstacles to create an environment conducive to sleep, including enlisting support of family members when necessary.

## Problem: Trouble Falling Asleep

*Question 1: Is the person consuming caffeine after noon?*
**Solution:** If yes, eliminate all forms of caffeine after noon.

*Question 2: What is the person doing before bed?*
**Solution:** Help the person develop a relaxing bedtime routine. Starting 30 to 60 minutes before bedtime, all work and stimulating activities need to end. Some people will need to turn off all devices with screens, either because of the stimulating nature of how most people use them, or because of sensitivity to the blue light frequencies that can disrupt circadian rhythm. If the person is exercising in the evening, try exercising in the morning. If the person is exercising in the morning, try evening. (If the person is not exercising at all, start with daily exercise—see Chapter 6.) There is no one single perfect prescription for the perfect bedtime routine; what works for one person will not work for someone else, so the goal is to help people discover what works for them.

## Problem: Not Staying Asleep

(Includes waking in the middle of the night and feeling wide awake or even having racing thoughts or feeling anxious, not being able to get back to sleep for a while, as well as waking up repeatedly, only sleeping lightly/dozing because of frequent waking.)

*Question 1: Is the person consuming any caffeine at any time of the day?*
**Solution:** If yes, eliminate caffeine. Switching to decaffeinated forms of favorite beverages is an acceptable alternative!

*Question 2: What does the person do if they wake up?*
**Solution:** Develop stress management and relaxation routines to follow and help restore a restful sleep pattern. If nocturia is a problem more than twice per night, have the person consult their doctor about the problem. Even though it is a common problem, it is not "normal."

# Optimal Physical Activity for Mental Health

Chapter

**6**

The amount of research showing that exercise benefits just about every mental health condition is significant. Despite that, most people still do not think of being physically active as a direct treatment for mood and cognitive disorders. People tend to think of exercise for weight loss or heart health, but not for brain health. But while physical activity is necessary not only for physical health, it is also necessary for mental health. The human brain functions better when the body is physically active.

## Depression and Exercise

There are numerous high quality studies on the effects of exercise on depression, and they overwhelmingly demonstrate effectiveness. A Cochrane review of 32 studies on exercise and depression show on average a "moderate" effect (Rimer et al., 2012). Six other studies compared exercise with cognitive behavioral therapy and found similar efficacy. What if the two therapies were combined, both exercise and cognitive behavioral therapy, or other psychology-based therapies, with demonstrated efficacy? It's possible there is a synergistic effect, and hopefully that study will be done.

## Anxiety and Exercise

The research on anxiety and exercise is not as overwhelmingly positive as it is for depression, meaning it is possible to find studies that show that anxiety was not helped by aerobic exercise. However, many of these trials used placebo treatments or other interventions that have been shown to have therapeutic benefit such as meditation, non-aerobic exercise such as yoga, cognitive behavioral therapy, and psycho-education. A meta-analysis of all these studies concluded that aerobic exercise does not benefit anxiety, but noted that the studies that used a "wait list" as the placebo instead of another active intervention did show benefit (Bartley, Hay & Block, 2013). A more accurate conclusion would be that aerobic exercise is beneficial, but not more beneficial than non-aerobic exercise or more beneficial than some forms of psychotherapy.

A different meta-analysis came to the opposite conclusion: "Exercise seems to be effective as an adjunctive treatment for anxiety disorders, but it is less effective compared with antidepressant treatment. Both aerobic and non-aerobic exercise seem to reduce anxiety symptoms. Social phobias may benefit from exercise when combined with group CBT.

Further well-conducted RCTs are needed" (Jayakody, Gunadasa & Hosker, 2014). Exercise is unlikely to completely eliminate the need for other forms of treatment in all cases, but, like depression, whether there is a synergistic effect when physical therapies are employed simultaneously with cognitive therapies and/or pharmaceutical therapies needs a great deal more study to be thoroughly understood.

## ADHD and Exercise

Most of the research on ADHD demonstrates that exercise is immediately helpful for people with ADHD. Just one aerobic activity session immediately improves both academic performance and behavior in children with ADHD as much as 30 percent (Ng, Ho, Chan, Yong & Yeo, 2017). Moderate to intense activity provided the most benefit. Some studies used no exercise as a control group, some used a group of age- and gender-matched volunteers who do not exhibit ADHD, and some used all four groups. It is important to note that both the ADHD groups and the non-ADHD groups demonstrated improvement in tasks or tests that require concentration after exercise, indicating that all humans benefit from aerobic activity. The fact that people with ADHD demonstrated a more dramatic improvement indicates that people with ADHD are more likely to suffer greater negative consequences from insufficient activity or a sedentary lifestyle.

## What Kind of Exercise is Best?

With the barrage of sound bites talking about exercise, saying things like, "Walking is as effective as running," "Higher intensity cardio leads to increased benefit," "Strength training is more important than cardio," "Yoga is safer than strength training," or "Yoga *is* strength-training," people get confused! What really is the best form of exercise?

The most important point of all these snippets of information is that *all* forms of activity have value. And all humans benefit from activity; **some is always better than none.** Even when people are recovering from surgery or injury, getting people up and moving is always a primary goal, almost immediately. People with specific medical conditions will need to work with their doctors and physical therapists about what is the best form and amount of activity for their situation, but the key is always to focus on what can be done, not what "can't" be done.

With the current epidemic of sedentary lifestyles, for the vast majority of people, more exercise would be better than what they are doing. So where to start? Start with what the person likes. Enjoying the activity is critical to long-term engagement; when exercise is just one more thing on the to-do list, it's not going to get done. Helping people find activities they truly enjoy that support their deeper life goals and priorities will foster long-term participation. If exercise was a drug, it would be a multi-billion dollar industry—everyone would be clamoring to buy it because it is so effective.

# Optimal Activity Level for Brain Health

**Optimal activity level for brain health requires two different types of activity: moderate amounts of low-intensity activity and short bursts of high-intensity activity.** While the following plan will not turn anyone into an athlete, it will change the brain chemistry in multiple ways that improve functioning and relieve the symptoms of mental illness.

# Active Lifestyle: 10,000 Steps a Day

The human body was designed to be active, and too much time spent sitting is damaging to health. To counter the effects of sitting, people do not even need to do anything that they usually think of as "exercise." They simply need to be up and about, rather than sitting or lying down. 10,000 steps per day (or more) is the goal. People do not need to go for five-mile power walks, but when they walk 10,000 steps throughout the day, the benefits add up over the day and over a lifetime.

Pedometers are a great tool for measuring this kind of activity, and at this point most people already own one—most cell phones can be used as pedometers, and many people with cell phones carry it with them already. Data shows that using pedometers increases people's activity level, so encourage the use of these tools. Some people will want to take it further with fancier devices that track not only steps taken but also heart rate, sleep quality, and other measures of health. There are other tools available for people who like those sorts of gadgets.

# High-Intensity Exercise Interval Routine

The other aspect of optimal activity level requires raising the heart rate. People don't need to figure out any equations of target heart rate to know if they are raising their heart rate enough, they simply need to engage in an activity that gets them out of breath. People can easily gauge when they are out of breath—and they cannot sustain that intensity level for long. So the key to high-intensity exercise is an interval routine: 30 seconds of high-intensity activity (that gets the person out of breath) followed by 90 seconds of a lower-intensity recovery activity. For example, a person may run to get out of breath, and then walk to recover. Add a four-minute warm-up at the beginning because people should not jump straight to high-intensity activity without some warm-up. This two-minute interval is repeated eight times. The total time for the routine is 20 minutes. People don't need to run marathons or go the gym for hours a day, but they do need to take 20 minutes and get their heart rate up.

The best part of the interval routine is that it is so easily customizable for each person's individual needs. Regardless of fitness level, physical limitations or injuries, and personal preference, everyone can find something that works for them. A person who likes going to the gym may use a treadmill or an elliptical trainer to do this kind of work out, and indeed those machines have these programs built right in to them. Every spin class is a variation on an interval routine. But if someone doesn't like going to the gym or doesn't have access to those machines, they can do it just by going outside and walking, running, or even jumping rope. Or if people prefer to stay inside, they can do a work-out video, many of which are free online and also incorporate strength training. It doesn't even have to be that structured; putting on music and dancing is a fun way to get the heart rate up, and get kids involved, too!

### Benefits of High-Intensity Exercise

When people move vigorously enough to get themselves out of breath, the benefits of that high-intensity exercise start immediately. It stimulates multiple physiological changes that affect mood and cognitive function. These effects begin during exercise, continue for hours to days after exercise, and build on each other day to day. The effects of daily exercise are cumulative.

One of the first responses to exercise is endorphin release. Endorphins diminish pain sensations and improve sleep quality. Many people have heard of the "runner's high." It is poorly understood and sometimes attributed to endorphins. Not everyone will experience something they would call a "high," but movement does make people report feeling happier in general. Improvements in sleep quality directly impact both mood and cognitive function in positive ways, both short- and long-term.

Exercise also stimulates neurotrophic release. Neurotrophins help the brain form new synaptic pathways and are involved in the formation of memories. Memory formation is part of learning, so increased neurotrophins enhance learning ability.

High-intensity exercise triggers multiple hormonal changes that benefit mood and energy levels. It stimulates thyroid function, which increases metabolism, improving mood and energy. High-intensity exercise also stimulates testosterone, which also improves mood and energy, benefiting both men and women.

Yet another benefit of exercise is improved adrenal function, which directly improves mood and ability to cope with stress. Better resilience to stress further improves mood, helping people break out of the cycle of feeling "stressed out."

## Tips for Getting Started and Long-Term Engagement

Ideally, people would engage in both low-and high-intensity activity six to seven days per week. But many people feel daunted by this, and may need to start out slower. Remember, some is always better than none, and work with people to change their routines in manageable ways. If every day sounds daunting, have people start with two to three days per week. The basic interval routine is 20 minutes, but it could be shortened to 10 minutes for people who are just starting out and still need to experience that their bodies really can do this. Even the busiest of people waste more than 20 minutes every day, so time can be made to fit this in.

Ideally, people would engage family or friends in the activity as well—exercise does not need to be a solo activity. (Though if someone has a regular habit of enjoying alone time or time away from other responsibilities while doing something active, that works, too!) When patients are struggling with too much to do, especially around family, help them combine priorities by making activity a part of social or family time. Not only does that reduce stress, the social engagement increases their enjoyment of the time and activity. It also enhances commitment—most people are much more likely to keep commitments made to other people than commitments to themselves only.

Setting goals, or even entering a competition, can also really inspire some people. Tracking progress and watching improvement helps them stay motivated. Having a structured plan, such as The Couch to 5K® plan or a 21-day fitness challenge, can also help people stay focused and learn how to break out of old habits and discover how much better they feel when they are active.

# Move Your Body!
## Boost Your Mood and Brain Power

Exercise is critical to maintain physical health *and* to keep your brain working at its best. Exercise improves mood, memory, the ability to learn and sleep, and the ability to handle stress.

### How much exercise is enough?

It depends on your unique health status, goals, and personal taste. Keep in mind the following:

1. First, pick something you enjoy doing. All movement is beneficial.
2. The positive effects of exercise start immediately, and accumulate with consistency.
3. Both high-and-low intensity activity benefit your brain in different ways.

### Goal 1: 10,000 steps per day

10,000 steps is the foundation of an active lifestyle. Here are some tips to get your daily steps in:

1. Use a pedometer app on your phone, or buy a pedometer at a sporting goods store.
2. Visit www.thewalkingsite.com/10000steps for tips and strategies.
3. If pain or injury are interfering, see a doctor about how to solve the problem.

### Goal 2: Raise your heart rate

Elevate your heart rate to the point of being out of breath. High intensity activity elevates mood, improves resilience to stress, and increases metabolism for days. Here's how to do it:

1. The only requirement is to choose an activity than can get you fully out of breath.
2. Do something you enjoy and find convenient.

3. Try this 20-minute interval plan:
   a. Start with a 4-minute low-intensity warm up.
   b. High-intensity activity for 30 seconds (any activity that gets you out of breath).
   c. Low-intensity recovery activity for 90 seconds.
   d. Repeat the 30-second activity burst followed by 90-second recovery *8 times*.

### *Goal 3: HAVE FUN with these exercise ideas*

- Gardening
- Hiking
- Walking
- Bicycling
- Kayaking
- Jumping rope
- Dancing
- Gyms
- Yoga
- Weights
- Online videos
- Swimming
- Spin classes

### Resources

Just about all of these programs can be modified to accommodate physical limitations. Physical therapists, yoga instructors, and personal trainers can give you valuable guidance. Always start by asking your doctor what kind of exercise is best for you.

# Food & Nutrition for Mental Health

*"It's better to pay the grocer than the doctor"* - Michael Pollan

This quote emphasizes two important points:

1. Failing to eat a healthy diet will cause a person to need a doctor, and the doctor will not be able to fix the problems caused by poor diet. No medication or surgery can correct the painful health conditions, both mental and physical, that result from poor diet.

2. Eating healthily requires not just knowledge, but also resources and effort. Teaching people how to eat is not just about food and nutrition, it also requires teaching people how to go about obtaining and preparing food, which includes learning how to shop for food and how to access assistance programs when needed. Doctors do not address these issues with patients, but direct these issues toward social workers and therapists.

There is a persistent myth that eating healthily is expensive. In fact, the opposite is true: Processed foods cost dramatically more than whole foods—the foods humans have been eating for millennia, the foods your great-great grandparents ate. **Whole foods are foods that are as fresh and as close to their natural state as possible, such as fresh fruit, vegetables, nuts, legumes, and whole grains.** Buying prepared food costs more than shopping at a grocery store. But shopping for whole foods requires teaching people a set of skills that is additional to educating them about nutrition. Knowing what to eat is only the first step; helping people make meaningful changes requires helping them overcome a variety of common obstacles to accessing and choosing healthy food.

Food quality also matters, and it is true that organic food does cost more. However, the first and *most important* step in eating healthily is eating food in the form it was grown. While organic broccoli is a small improvement over non-organic broccoli, eating non-organic broccoli is a *huge* improvement over not eating broccoli at all. Too often, people get seduced by organic junk foods, but they are still junk foods. Organic corn chips are still a highly processed food that is best avoided. When people are already eating a whole foods diet, and can afford organic food, that is the next step. The first step, for everyone, is to save money by eating whole foods.

Another aspect of food quality is freshness. Ideally, everyone would eat vegetables harvested that day from their own garden or by their local farmer. Obviously this is not a modern reality for most people at most times. When people are ready, encouraging them to explore their local farmer's markets and community-sponsored agriculture (CSA) programs can open up a whole new community and introduce them to a new way of finding high-quality, affordable produce. But the reality is, grocery stores supply the bulk of the food people buy, and frozen vegetables are a convenient, effective way to make high-quality produce available at all times.

When produce has to be transported large distances, fresh produce is picked early, decreasing its nutrient content, and then various chemicals are used to delay ripening for transport. Produce that is frozen tends to be picked at the height of the season, when there is surplus supply, and then transported a much shorter distance to the facility that freezes it, and then it can be shipped longer distances more easily. In many cases, especially in the winter northern climates, frozen food can actually contain greater nutritional value than the fresh produce available at that time.

## Healthy Diet is Not Just About Nutrients

The rest of this chapter, and the whole next section, are going to talk extensively about the nutrients in food and the role they play in mental health. However, no single nutrient will ever "solve the problem." Nor will eating any particular "superfood" be the whole answer. Humans require a complex array of nutrients to maintain homeostasis. Some of these nutrients we know about, but likely there are some that have not been discovered yet because there are numerous compounds that we eat every day that scientists are just starting to understand the importance of. The science of nutrition is young, and new advances are being made every day.

These constant new advances are part of the reason why people hear about nutrition and food changes. Sometimes they contradict other "truths." Some of these evolutions of knowledge will be explained in the specifics of later chapters. But there is another, darker reason that nutritional claims so often contradict each other. The complex science of nutrition is often diluted into a single fact or soundbite, and soundbites rarely convey the true reality of an issue. Rather, they focus on one particular side and emphasize that point, often taking facts out of context and distorting the deeper truth.

This process has been used in marketing to make foods appear healthier than they are. Sadly, the vast majority of health "information" that Americans are exposed to is not put out by doctors or scientists or anyone who is trying to help people improve their health. Most health claims are made with one goal: to convince people to buy a product. Claiming a product is healthy has been shown to be an extremely effective sales strategy, but many of these claims are misleading because they focus on only part of a truth.

This continual exposure to health misinformation leaves people at best confused, and at worst deceived. People who are truly trying to eat healthily get frustrated when they fail to get results because what they thought was healthy actually is not healthy at all. The confusion that comes from hearing contradictory advice leads some people to think it does not matter what they eat, or that no one really knows what is really healthy so why bother. Helping people navigate these constant obstacles and learn what actually is a healthy diet is one of the single most important ways clinicians can help their clients.

# What is a Healthy Diet?

The single best soundbite of advice comes from Michael Pollan (2008): *"Eat food, not too much, mostly plants."* This phrase sums up all of the most important points regarding how to eat in a way that promotes health. But even this simple, straightforward statement requires quite a bit of explanation because too many people no longer even know what "real food" even is.

Over the past several decades, the food industry has changed many of the most common foods dramatically by adding various chemicals to extend shelf life and enhance texture and taste, and removing certain parts of foods that are deemed less appealing. But these artificial chemicals, additives, and preservatives have dramatically modified what Americans consider to be "food." Until this century, yogurt was made by adding certain bacteria to milk, and controlling the environment in a way that allowed the bacteria to transform the milk into a creamy, though often somewhat lumpy, texture. Now, yogurt is made by adding numerous chemicals to milk that transform it into the homogenous, pudding-like texture that most people think of as yogurt today. However, the nutritional content of each of those different substances is so drastically different that they should not go by the same name. Traditionally-made yogurt does have certain nutritional benefits; however, what most people call yogurt bears little resemblance to what our grandparents would have called yogurt, and not only has zero health benefits, but it actually contributes to many health problems. Even most "Greek" yogurt is so loaded with sugar and chemicals that eating it should be considered risky. Only plain yogurt is truly yogurt, and the only yogurt that can be considered healthy.

For a more in-depth history of the evolution of food and how we came to be steeped in so much contradiction, read Michael Pollan's book, *The Omnivore's Dilemma* (2007). His research details the progression of how the conversation shifted away from food toward nutrients, opening the door for the development of what he terms "edible food-like substances."

The combination of eating these chemicals, which have variable and poorly understood impacts on health, combined with *not* eating the foods humans evolved to eat has created a whole new class of diseases called "the western diseases" that were previously very rare, but are now epidemic.

Mental health is not typically what people think of first when they think about diseases that are due to poor diet, but without proper nutrition the brain cannot function. The brain needs a steady supply of nutrients to work properly, and when those nutrients are out of balance, it causes symptoms. Section 3 will go into more specific detail on those connections. But focusing on certain individual nutrients will never be the whole answer—a working brain requires broad nutrition from a variety of healthy foods.

A critical part of helping people make better food choices is to teach them to be skeptical of advertised health claims. If a food is advertised as healthy, it is probably less healthy than many other foods. The healthiest foods, such as vegetables, typically don't have marketing budgets, while processed foods do. **Even if it is just a label proclaiming the food is healthy, chances are it has been processed in a way that actually makes it**

**less healthy than many whole foods in their natural state.** For practical advice on how to escape the hypocrisy of modern food marketing, read Michael Pollan's sequels: *In Defense of Food: An Eater's Manifesto* (2008) and *Food Rules: An Eater's Manual* (2009).

## Start With Vegetables

The end of the phrase, "[eat] mostly plants," all too often gets overlooked in the current diet wars. So much emphasis is put on whether or not to eat meat or whether paleo or vegan is healthier that people often lose sight of the basis of *both* of those diets. In both diets, the staple foods are vegetables. Either one can be distorted to technically fit the "rules" but have almost nothing left of the original intent of the diet. **Regardless of whether someone eats meat or not, what the vast majority of humans have evolved to eat is a diet based on vegetables.** The only near-universal dietary advice for all humans is to eat vegetables. (The statistics on how many Americans eat no vegetables at all is horrifying.) This is so important that, for the vast majority of people, simply eating more vegetables would improve their nutrient intake (and help them lose weight).

The most important part of helping people change their diets is understanding where they are starting. Many people say, "I don't like vegetables." Just telling them to eat vegetables is not going to work. Ask them what it means to them to eat vegetables, and help them explore new ways of preparing vegetables that may be far more appetizing. *Nobody* likes plain canned veggies that have been microwaved. The key to learning to eat vegetables includes learning different ways to cook them, or find them prepared by someone else. The following handout can provide a framework for working with people around trying new options and expanding their palates.

Even if people say they eat veggies, it is important to discuss how many veggies they are eating, knowing that the concept of a "serving" is all but useless. All too often people think of vegetables more as a side dish than the main part of meal—ideally half of all meals are vegetables. At a restaurant, I once ordered the fish special that came with "seasonal vegetables." The vegetables turned out to be two stalks of asparagus, five green beans, and two baby carrots. They were arranged very nicely on the plate, but half that plate should have been seasonal vegetables!

# Eat Your Vegetables

What is in a healthy diet? With all the fad diet wars, it is more confusing than ever to know what to eat. But there is one fundamental food that all these diets agree on: *vegetables*.

**How much is enough?**
Half your dinner plate should be vegetables, six nights per week. Regardless of whether you eat paleo, vegan, low fat, or low carb, make half your dinner plate vegetables.

**Lunch**
For lunch, have a salad six days per week. Salad for lunch is the backbone of a healthy diet. Other lunch ideas to get your vegetables include:

1. Use greens, seasonal vegetables, and chicken, fish, beans and/or tofu.
2. Always include protein such as grilled chicken or salmon half the size of your palm.
3. If you prefer vegetarian options, include a cup of spiced beans or some grilled tofu.
4. Soup that is full of vegetables works too and is an enjoyable alternative for winter.

**Dinner**
We often think of vegetables as the side dish. But really, they should be the main event on our dinner plates. For dinner, half of your plate should be vegetables. Use these tips for dinner:

1. Make half your dinner plate vegetables.
2. Use seasonal vegetables for better taste and nutrition.
3. Find 3 new vegetable recipes to try each month to keep it interesting.
4. Don't be afraid to repeat your favorite vegetable dishes! Often!

**Resources**

The best vegetables to eat:

- Kale
- Collard greens
- Chard
- Mustard greens
- Spinach
- Arugula
- Romaine lettuce
- Red leaf lettuce
- Green lettuce
- Broccoli
- Cauliflower
- Parsnips
- Turnips
- Carrots
- Onions
- Garlic
- Asparagus
- Artichokes
- Celery
- Squash
- Yams
- Sweet potatoes

## CASE STUDY
# Bipolar Nutrition

Robert presented with a diagnosis of bipolar with psychotic features and had been hospitalized four times over the previous year. New medications had been started with every hospitalization, and when he came to me he was on two mood stabilizing medications, both at over maximum dose, three anti-psychotic medications at maximum dose, and a benzodiazepine for sleep. He was barely capable of holding a conversation, but his family had not given up on him. His parents recounted the repeated suffering of the last few years, and how painful it was that their formally-successful 40-year-old son had ended up living on the streets.

When I asked Robert what he ate, he said, "M&M's." When I asked him why he didn't eat any other food, he responded that he liked M&M's, and he didn't have anything else. When I asked if he would be willing to eat other food if someone gave it to him, he initially asked why and said that candy tastes better than other food.

It took some coaxing, but I eventually convinced him to try eating what his parents would provide him. I knew it wouldn't solve everything, but I knew nothing could be solved without getting nutrients into him. He didn't want to take any more pills because he "already took too many."

His parents also agreed to the plan—it would be a green protein smoothie for breakfast, a sandwich for lunch that was made on sprouted grain bread and had to contain both a meat and a vegetable, and dinner was going to be a source of protein and vegetables.

Six months later, Robert had not been hospitalized, was down to two medications and looking for a job. He was able to hold a conversation and take care of his basic needs again. He was by no means "cured;" likely, Robert would always benefit from medication. But instead of swinging back and forth between thinking that the medications would save him or were the source of the problem, he now better understood what he had to do to keep his body in balance, to not end up feeling over-medicated and terrible. Six months is not long enough to establish stability, but it did appear that the worst of the cycle he had slipped into was broken.

Over the next five years, Robert did get a job and was able to support himself. Even with better self-care, he continued to benefit from two medications—when the dose was lowered, symptoms would increase, and he was able to gain a whole new understanding of how the medications affected him.

Not every case can be cured by nutrition alone; in fact, many won't be cured by nutrition alone. But nutrition plays a role in *every* case, so even in cases of extreme symptoms and suffering, always evaluate the roles the basics are playing and make sure they are being addressed; medications will never be the whole answer either.

## Snack Smart

Another area of eating where most Americans can make tremendous change in their nutrition with just a little bit of effort is around snacking. It is extremely common for people to snack on foods that are high in calories and chemicals and low in nutritional value. **Simply switching to eating "real" foods for snacks, foods like raw nuts, fruits, and veggies, can dramatically change both mood and ability to focus.** Snacking smart is a "big bang for your buck" switch.

Often, people say things like, "I have no willpower." But willpower is 10 percent knowing what your body needs, and 90 percent being prepared to give it what it needs. *Nobody* has willpower when they are over-tired or over-hungry. Everybody is more prone to visiting the vending machine, stopping for fast food, or just having a couple extra pieces of candy found on a co-worker's desk at these times. The key to avoiding those situations is being prepared with healthy snacks and eating them before it's too late.

The following handout will help people better understand themselves and develop strategies that truly work for them. There is no one perfect strategy that works for everyone, and typically, this process will require a deeper exploration of the person's obstacles to caring for themselves. Most people will need help overcoming these obstacles, and ongoing support during that process is usually the difference between success and repeated failure. The 10 percent education part is only the tip of the iceberg—the real work comes in figuring out how to be prepared. While snacking is an effective place to start, it's only part of a person's overall relationship with food, and most people will benefit from a more comprehensive strategy.

# Snack Smart

When changing how you eat, "snacking smart" gives you the most reward for the least effort. Eating the foods that have been heavily marketed as snack foods, such as chips, crackers, and granola bars, is a very common reason for feeling lethargic, spacey, unfocused, anxious, and irritable. Snacking on nutritious foods will break the cycle of feeling and eating poorly.

**Should I snack?**
You might worry that snacking will cause you to gain weight. It's true; *unhealthy* snacking is a major source of the extra, empty calories that cause obesity. But avoiding snacking may be causing you to overeat at meals. Instead of straining your body to not eat, strengthen your body by giving it the foods it needs when it needs them.

Answer the following questions to determine if and when smart snacking will work for you.

1. Do you eat between meals?
2. Are you overweight?
3. Do you ever have food cravings?
4. Do you ever feel shaky, lightheaded, woozy, or dizzy for no apparent reason?

If you answered yes to any of these questions, smart snacking is going to be critical for feeling your best.

## Preparation

The key to snacking smart is preparation. A few minutes of preparation can save you hours of suffering. Particularly if you feel you lack will power around food, try eating a healthy snack *before* you start to feel hungry.

1. Eat snacks that provide protein, essential fats, and fiber.
2. Snack every 3 to 4 hours after a meal (every 2 hours for children).
3. Plan a meal and snack schedule.
4. Use your phone alarm to keep to your schedule.
5. Prep healthy snacks for the week and grab them every morning before leaving.

## Resources

Make snacking easy and try these three smart snacks:

1. 2 tablespoons of raw walnuts, pecans, or cashews (or a mix) and a piece of fresh fruit
2. Veggies (such as carrots, peppers, celery, tomatoes) and 1/4 cup of hummus
3. Half a sandwich: Chicken/turkey, lettuce, and other veggies on 100% whole or sprouted grain bread

## Food is More Than the Sum of Its Nutrients

It goes without saying that eating is essential for life. But the physical nutrients in food are only one of many reasons that humans eat. Eating feeds essential social, cultural, and spiritual parts of life as well, and these aspects of eating are just as important as the physical nutrition. Because people have different physical needs as well as different social environments, there is no one perfect diet for all people. Developing truly healthy eating habits requires addressing not just the physical nutrition found in food, but also the emotional nourishment that comes from both food and enjoying eating.

A comprehensive strategy requires addressing *all* of these relationships with food. Some people are already very aware of many of these relationships, but for many people, they live in the subconscious. They often underlie many of the obstacles people face when trying to eat in a more healthy way, and addressing those obstacles will bring these issues to the surface. Therefore, helping people make healthier food choices requires helping them better understand their relationships with food.

> **Improving people's relationships with food and helping them learn to value food and enjoy eating in a whole new way is fundamentally about helping them learn a whole new level of self-care.**

If "eating healthily" becomes one more thing on the to-do list that stresses them out or that results in feelings of failure, long-term change simply won't happen. Rarely does the latest diet plan/book/program yield lasting results. While those resources provide the "what to do" and "how to do it," they rarely address deeper relationships. Only when these deeper issues are addressed, with ongoing support, will people reach a new level. Doctors are not trained to deal with these issues, but mental health professionals are.

Most people do need and benefit from physical resources that provide some guidance and structure for where to start and what to do. The following handouts can help start the conversation and help people find the resources that work best for them. My personal experience as a doctor has been that when I recommend specific resources, people return and tell me everything they don't like about that particular plan. But sometimes they would find something different to use, and over the years I came to realize that it was less about the differences in the plans and more about the process of finding them. Quite simply, most people don't like to be told what to do! But when they invest in finding something that works for them, and use it with professional guidance to customize it and make it their own, they are much more likely to fully engage with the process and benefit from it.

One particular aspect of this process that deserves emphasis: there is no one perfect plan for everyone. Part of the reason there are so many diets and plans that come and go is because different people need different resources. Some people do say things like, "Just tell me what to eat." For those people, a meal plan works well. Having the instructions to follow (breakfast, lunch, dinner, and snacks) is actually comforting and stress-relieving. The structure gives them a place to start, helps them stick with it, and always gives them a clear place to come back to. Meal plans that provide shopping lists help them stay organized and prepared, another key factor to changing habits long-term.

But other people *hate* the idea of following a meal plan. It feels too restrictive and rigid and interferes with their enjoyment of food. They simply won't do it. Those people need a different kind of strategy for being mindful of their food choices that still allows for spontaneity and creativity. Food journaling, or counting sugar, fat, calories or even "points," are typically a better strategy choice in these cases. All of those tools help people be more mindful of what they eat and help people discover the hidden patterns in their food choices. Awareness, along with the right support, can be a powerful combination that helps people finally get where they want to go.

The most important place to start with all people is around building their support network. Clinicians are only one small part of the critical support network that people need to make significant long-term change. When people face criticism of new habits, or if friends, family, and co-workers are constantly tempting them back to old habits, it is nearly impossible to build new habits. Helping people navigate the difficulties of enlisting useful support from the people closest to them is another way that mental health professionals can dramatically shift people's abilities to improve their nutrition.

Another important aspect for both clinicians and clients to keep in mind is that change does not happen overnight. Expecting too much and then getting discouraged is one of the most common reasons for failure. Another is simply trying to change too much at once. For some people, a major reset, such as a juice cleanse, can be invigorating and motivating. But for other people, changing everything at once is overwhelming and counterproductive. More often, starting small and being consistent is what will yield the most long-term benefit. Starting simple habits, like taking a break to eat, will help people be more mindful of what they eat and how much they eat. People take breaks for all sorts of reasons, but all too often eat while doing something else—driving, sitting in a meeting, watching TV. Stop what you are doing and take four deep breaths before starting to eat. Focus on chewing each bite thoroughly—count to 13 if necessary. Starting with these little habits will help people build better habits and continue them long-term.

# Prepare Your Way to Food Willpower

Countless people feel they have no willpower over poor food choices. If you fall into this group, you may have imbalanced brain chemistry that results from eating the wrong foods. The hardest part of willpower is getting started - but as you follow through, you will find it gets easier instead of harder. You'll also experience just how much better you feel when you choose to eat healthily.

**Keys to maintaining your food willpower:**

1. Choose a meal plan strategy

2. Build a support network—enlist a friend, family member, co-worker, or therapist

3. Prepare healthy foods

4. Set phone alarms to remind you to eat on time

5. Eat before you get too hungry

6. Stick with it—it only gets easier with time!

**Decide on a strategy**

Does the thought of deciding what to eat stress you out? Develop a meal plan! Refer to the Resources list below for meal plan ideas.

If the thought of a meal plan leaves you feeling trapped, bored, or uninspired, then skip it! Instead, simply write down what you eat. Food journaling is the single best way to improve mindfulness around eating and the choices you make. To get started, gather your favorite recipes that fit well into your chosen strategy, and find a few new ones to try as well.

### Resources

Meal plan examples can be found in these resources. If creating a meal plan is too overwhelming by yourself, enlist the help of a qualified therapist, nutritionist, or physician.

- South Beach Diet (Maintenance Phase)
- www.fresh20.com
- *Grain Brain* by Dr. David Perlmutter

### Tools for tracking what you eat:

1. www.weightwatchers.com or join a Weight Watchers meeting
2. www.myfitnesspal.com
3. www.loseit.com

# Start Smart with Breakfast

Undoubtedly you have heard, "Breakfast is the most important meal of the day." But why? What makes breakfast important is that it either strengthens your body or strains your body, and the effects of either last throughout the day.

A balanced breakfast is the mental health equivalent of gathering your tools to take with you for the day's tasks. It gives your body the raw materials it needs to make the neurotransmitters and hormones that keep your body working at its best, including balanced blood sugar and a working immune system. When you give your body a sugary breakfast cereal, or skip breakfast entirely, it triggers stress hormones, and excess inflammation, making it harder for your body to function well. It also causes blood sugar swings, leading to mood swings and poor focus.

### Tips to start right
1. Choose 1 or 2 breakfast options that you like and prepare them ahead of time.
2. Eat within 3 hours of waking or when you first start to feel hungry, whichever comes first.

### Resources
The only reason we think of cereal for breakfast is because food companies have spent millions of dollars telling us to eat it for breakfast. Below are the top three options for a healthy breakfast that fuels you up for the day:

1. Veggie and chicken sausage omelet with 2 slices of Ezekiel toast
2. Breakfast smoothie
3. Dinner leftovers—turn your healthy dinner into a healthy breakfast!

# The Power of Hydration

Drinking adequate amounts of water is a critical part of a whole foods diet. Without adequate water, the biochemical processes that keep you alive and feeling good simply do not work as well, interfering with both mood and cognitive function.

**How much should you drink?**
You have likely heard the instruction to drink eight glasses (64 ounces total) of water per day. This recommendation is easy to remember and effective for the average person. The more exact guideline is to drink 1/2 ounce for every pound of body weight. The table below shows how much water you should drink by your body weight.

| Your Body Weight | Number of Glasses | Total Water |
|---|---|---|
| 80 pounds | 5 glasses | 40 oz |
| 100 pounds | 6 glasses | 50 oz |
| 120 pounds | 7.5 glasses | 60 oz |
| 140 pounds | 9 glasses | 70 oz |
| 160 pounds | 10 glasses | 80 oz |
| 180 pounds | 11 glasses | 90 oz |
| 200 pounds | 12.5 glasses | 100 oz |
| 220 pounds | 14 glasses | 110 oz |
| 240 pounds | 15 glasses | 120 oz |
| 260 pounds | 16 glasses | 130 oz |
| 280 pounds | 17.5 glasses | 140 oz |
| 300 pounds | 19 glasses | 150 oz |

The best way to tell if you are drinking enough water is looking at the color of your urine—it should be clear. If you see yellow, drink more water!

### What should you drink?

Do all fluids count, or only pure water? Not all fluids affect hydration and overall function the same way. **What you drink is as important as what you eat.** Below are the top three drinks:

1. Pure water—invest in a water filter to improve the flavor of city water
2. Herbal tea—just as healthy as water with countless numbers of flavors
3. Seltzer—the fizzy kick without the sugar, sweeteners, and caffeine

### Hydration tip

Start each morning with 16 ounces of lemon water. Squeeze 1/4 fresh lemon into hot or cold water to stimulate detoxification and digestion.

# Simple Substitutions

A few simple substitutions can dramatically increase the nutrients you consume.

**Buy Ezekiel bread or 100% whole grain bread**
Ezekiel bread is a sprouted grain bread. This means that instead of grinding the grain into a flour, which depletes the nutrient content, the grain is sprouted and then made into bread. The sprouting process makes the nutrients much more available. Most people who feel bloated or lethargic after eating regular bread stop experiencing those uncomfortable symptoms when they switch to Ezekiel bread.

**Cook with olive oil and coconut oil**
The best oils to cook with are coconut oil and olive oil because they do not become toxic when heated. Other liquid oils break down into carcinogens when heated. Anytime you put oil in a pan for sautéing or frying, use coconut oil or olive oil. Choose coconut oil when cooking at higher heats. When making salad dressings, use olive oil. Read labels on prepared foods and choose those that are made with olive oil or coconut oil.

Eliminate all hydrogenated or partially hydrogenated oils, of any kind, and avoid vegetable oil, corn oil, and soy oil.

**Easy substitution tips**
1.  Always read labels on bread.
2.  Choose breads that are 100% whole grain, meaning the first ingredient needs to be "whole wheat flour" (or another form of whole grain flour if you need to avoid gluten).
3.  Replace cooking oils with coconut oil and olive oil.

# Specific Nutrient Deficiencies that Commonly Contribute to Mental Health Symptoms

The last chapter covered how to eat a healthy, whole foods diet, but why is eating healthily so important? Most people have a sense that "eating right" is something they *should* do, or they may have a vague belief that it will give them the nutrients they need to maintain health. But actually identifying and understanding what those nutrients are and how they work in the body gives people a much deeper appreciation and motivation for why eating healthily is important and how to make the choices that most benefit their health.

This section will provide more detailed information on the nutritional deficiencies that most commonly cause mental health symptoms.

# Fats: Discerning the Good from the Bad for Mental Health

People tend to have a lot of misconceptions around fat for two reasons:

1. There are a lot of different kinds of fats, and it is complicated to keep straight how they all relate to each other.
2. The current information on fat directly contradicts what was believed about fat a few decades ago.

The following chart illustrates how the different kinds of fats relate to each other. The headings at the top are the major categories of fat, and each column contains examples of that kind of fat. Labeling a fat good or bad is usually an oversimplification, but it does help people develop a feel for the directions they should be heading. Dark grey boxes are bad fats, white outlined boxes are good fats, and light grey boxes means "proceed with caution." The proceed with caution fats mean people need to eat some of these, but Americans typically eat way too much of them and that imbalance causes health problems.

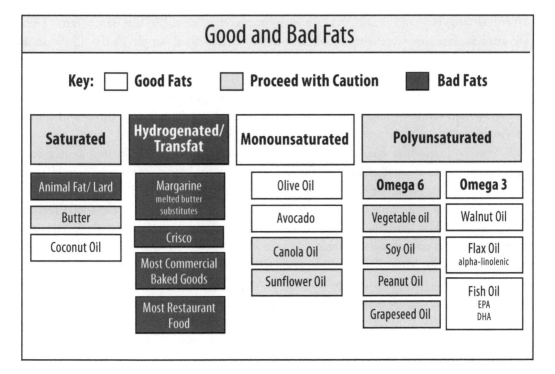

## Saturated Fats

Examples of foods that are predominantly saturated fat are animal fat, lard, butter, and coconut oil. The reason saturated fats as a column are in the light grey box is because even though some saturated fat is necessary for optimal brain function, Americans as a population tend to eat much more saturated fat than they should, and suffer health issues because of it. For most people, the excess saturated fat is in the form of animal fat, which is why animal fat and lard are in dark grey box. (Lard is simply animal fat in its pure form.)

Coconut oil is shown in white outlined box because coconut oil has been demonstrated to not have some of the negative health effects of excess animal fat (Feranil, Duazo, Kuzawa, & Adair, 2011). Coconut oil also contains medium chain triglycerides, which benefit   digestion, immune function, and metabolism (Assunção, Ferreira, dos Santos, Cabral, & Florêncio, 2009; Seaton, Welle, Warenko, & Campbell, 1986; St-Onge, Ross, Parsons, & Jones, 2003). For these reasons, getting fat from coconut oil is preferred to animal fat or butter.

One beneficial characteristic of saturated fats is their ability to withstand the high heat of cooking. Polyunsaturated fats break down and turn carcinogenic when exposed to high heat. Saturated fats are more resistant to these changes, and therefore, when cooking with high heat, saturated fats are the healthiest fats to use.

Of course, saturated fats still need to be used in moderation; this does not mean using large amounts of saturated fats is healthy. The best approach is to use small amounts of coconut oil or other saturated fat when cooking with high heat, and keep other sources of saturated fat (beef, cheese) in balance with the other forms of fat the body needs.

## Hydrogenated Fats (Trans Fats)

Hydrogenated fats and trans fats are two terms that refer to the same fats. These are artificial fats that were introduced into the American food supply in the 1980s in an attempt to reduce the amount of saturated fat in processed food. At that time, it was thought that these fats were a healthier alternative, but once that theory was finally tested, it turned out not to be true. In fact, studies show that hydrogenated fats are actually *more damaging* than saturated fats. This is why the whole column is dark grey boxes and should be avoided.

Pure hydrogenated fats are various forms of margarine. This revelation is not new; many people have avoided margarine for decades or more. Many people who would never buy a tub of margarine are still consuming significant amounts of hydrogenated fats in baked goods and restaurant foods. These fats continue to be used in these foods for one simple reason: They are cheaper. So while not all baked goods contain these fats, and many restaurants do not use saturated fats, the least expensive baked goods and restaurant options usually do. Most of the baked goods (muffins, cakes, cookies) and crackers on sale at a typical grocery store contain hydrogenated fats. Generally, fast food restaurants still use these fats. Therefore, avoiding hydrogenated fats (trans fats) requires not just avoiding margarine, but also avoiding processed food and some restaurant food. Legislation in some parts of the country is changing around the use of these fats, and hopefully, this section will be obsolete soon. But until then, people need to read labels.

Because butter is more expensive and needs to be used sparingly, many people are still looking for butter substitutes, but they don't want them to contain hydrogenated fats. The food industry has responded to this and there are now many butter substitutes available that do not contain hydrogenated fats. Reading labels carefully is still critical—some of these products still contain trans fats but make it look like they don't. People need to ignore the claims made on the front of the package and carefully read the ingredient list. If there are "hydrogenated" or "partially-hydrogenated" fats, those are the trans fats. Nutrition labels now break out trans fats as its own category, so the number there needs to be zero.

Another reason to carefully read the labels of these products is to look for the variety of chemicals that are often used to replace these fats. The best fats to eat are in their natural form, without adding a lot of additional ingredients to change the texture. Chemical preservatives such as THBQ, BHA, BHT, and calcium disodium EDTA can be avoided by comparing labels on different brands.

## Monounsaturated Fats

Monounsaturated fats are truly in the middle between saturated fats and polyunsaturated fats because they share properties of both. Saturated fats require higher temperatures to melt, whereas polyunsaturated fats remain liquid, even at cold (refrigerator) temperatures. Monounsaturated are in the middle—liquid at room temperature, solid in the refrigerator.

Because monounsaturated fats are more similar to saturated fats than polyunsaturated fats, they are the next best kind of oil to cook with. While they do not stand up to heat as well as saturated fats, they do withstand the heat of cooking much better than the polyunsaturated fats. When it comes to cooking, the further left on the chart, the better;  further to the right, the worse the fat is. The polyunsaturated fats, and particularly the  omega-3 types of polyunsaturated fats, should never be heated.

This is why olive oil has been so frequently recommended as a good oil to cook with. It is at the top of the list in a white outlined box because, of all the monounsaturated fats, it is the most purely monounsaturated fat. These labels (and therefore columns) are over-simplified. These pure plant oils don't contain only one kind of oil. Plant oils are naturally mixtures of different kinds of fats and are labeled by the dominant one. All the oils in the monounsaturated column are over 50 percent monounsaturated fats, but they all contain other kinds of fat as well. Olive oil has more monounsaturated fat and less polyunsaturated fat than safflower oil or canola oil, which is why olive oil is in the white outlined box on the top, while safflower and canola are listed in the light grey boxes.

## Polyunsaturated Fats

The two major categories of polyunsaturated fats are omega-6 and omega-3. Both are "essential fatty acids," which means humans need to eat them. Without adequate omega-6 and omega-3, the human brain (and body) will not function properly. The reason the omega-6 column is in the light grey box and the omega-3 column is in a white outlined box is because most Americans eat too much omega-6, but not enough omega-3.

Because people truly need omega-6, telling people to avoid omega-6 is actually poor advice. (Beware of foods that have started to advertise "low omega-6" as a health claim.) The most useful dietary guidance is helping people understand which foods contain omega-3 and how to get them into their diet. Eating more omega-3 will not only restore the deficiency, it will usually also reduce the amount of omega-6 consumption. This, along with cooking with the right oils, will move people toward eating the right balance of fats.

## Omega-3 Fats

Nuts and seeds are the plant-based sources of omega-3 fats. Walnuts are the best nut source. Flax seeds are the richest plant-based source of omega-3, meaning flax oil has the most omega-3 per drop. Flax seeds contain many other nutrients in addition to the oil, so eating the entire seed does have some advantages; however, it must be ground up before being eaten!

> **The hull of whole flax seeds cannot be digested by humans, so unless the seed has been ground up, it passes through the human digestive tract untouched, and the nutrients are not accessible.**

Fish oil is also listed as a source of omega-3 fats. The reason fish oil gets so much more attention medically than the other forms of omega-3 is because fish oil contains eicosapentaenoic acid, known as EPA, and docosahexaenoic acid, known as DHA. EPA and DHA are the omega-3 forms the body actually uses. The form of omega-3 found in nuts and seeds is alpha-linolenic acid, known as ALA.

EPA and DHA can be made from ALA, so it is possible for a person to be healthy while eating a purely plant-based diet. However, if the pathway that converts ALA to EPA and DHA is not working, it is possible for a person to be EPA- and DHA-deficient even if they are eating adequate nuts and seeds. The two major causes for not being able to convert ALA to EPA and DHA are inadequate nutrients and exposure to heavy metals or cigarette smoke.

Therefore, eating nuts and seeds alone is not enough for the body to make adequate EPA and DHA; people also need to eat a variety of other nutritious foods such as vegetables and whole grains to ensure adequate supplies of the niacin (vitamin B3), pyridoxine (vitamin B6), magnesium, and zinc necessary for the conversion. Exposure to cigarette smoke, heavy metals, or high amounts of alcohol will also interfere with the enzymes that make the conversion and lead to EPA/DHA deficiency if the person does not eat fish.

## Why are EPA and DHA so Important?

EPA and DHA are critical to proper cell membrane functioning. Every cell in the human body has a cell membrane, which separates the contents of the cell from the rest of the body. This membrane contains the receptors that are critical to cellular communication.

All the messengers that the body uses to communicate with other parts of the body need to bind to receptors for that message to be "read" properly. The body has a variety of these messengers, which affect all aspects of physical and mental health, but two critical examples of these messengers are hormones and neurotransmitters. When a person is deficient in EPA and DHA, neurotransmitters cannot bind properly. Symptoms of neurotransmitter deficiency are not always due to lack of neurotransmitters. Sometimes the neurotransmitters are there in appropriate amounts, but if the cells that need them cannot bind them, the symptoms of deficiency occur anyway. This is why EPA and DHA therapy has been shown to be beneficial in several diseases that involve neurotransmitter disruptions—bipolar disorder (Saunders et al., 2016), ADHD (Sonuga-Barke et al., 2013), and depression (Sarris, 2017).

One particularly exciting study (Amminger et al., 2015) shows that EPA and DHA can potentially prevent psychosis. In a placebo-controlled study of 81 adolescents who were assessed with extremely high risk of psychosis, the treatment group was given 12 weeks of supplemental EPA at 700mg and DHA at 480mg. At the one-year follow-up, nine months after the intervention had ended, the treatment group showed a significantly lower rate of having transitioned to a full psychotic disorder. But the most exciting part of this research is the long-term follow-up, which happened 6.7 years later. (Six years is an extremely rare length of time to follow up on medical intervention; usually it is much shorter, particularly in mental health research.) At 6.7 years, 9.8 percent of the treatment group versus 40 percent of the placebo group had converted to a psychotic disorder. This is the first and only intervention that has ever been shown to potentially prevent psychosis. No drug has ever yielded anything even close. In a more complete evaluation, 53 percent of the treatment group had met the criteria for an Axis-1 disorder during the 6.7 years, versus 83 percent of the placebo group. Further, in the treatment group, only 6.7 percent showed severe impairment and 70 percent were employed full-time.

This study still leaves many questions unanswered, but it does show how important and exciting future research on EPA and DHA is. Exactly how much EPA/DHA is enough and when the most critical development times are for adequate EPA and DHA is still unknown. But what is clear is that EPA and DHA are critical for healthy brain function, at all stages of life, including childhood and adolescence.

## Sources of EPA and DHA

While many people are aware that fish oil is readily available and aggressively marketed in pill form, people do not need to take pills to get EPA and DHA. As with all nutrients, eating the foods that supply the nutrients we need is always preferable to taking supplements.

Fish are the richest sources of EPA and DHA, but not all fish oils are EPA and DHA, so only certain fish are rich sources of EPA and DHA. The fish with the most EPA and DHA per bite are:

- Salmon
- Halibut
- Mackerel
- Krill

But even within a species of fish, not all are equal. The majority of salmon available in the U.S. today is farm-raised. Farm-raised salmon, often called Atlantic salmon, is not fed the same food they would be eating in their wild environment. When salmon do not eat the algae that provide EPA and DHA, they cannot accumulate the EPA and DHA in their bodies, and therefore, will not contain as much. Wild salmon, usually Alaskan salmon, still live in their natural environment and do eat the algae that provides EPA and DHA.

If someone was to use salmon alone to meet their EPA/DHA requirements, they would need to eat a four to six ounce portion, two to three times per week. But a wiser, more balanced approach would be to eat salmon one to two times per week and also eat a variety of nuts, seeds, and vegetables on a daily basis. This approach would provide the omega-3 fats that are turned into EPA/DHA by other nutrients found in vegetables, as well as providing other nutrition.

However, not all nuts are the same either. Walnuts and pecans have the most omega-3 fats. Peanuts have none, and should not be considered a source of omega-3 fats. Ground flax seeds are the richest plant-based source of omega-3, but flax seeds must be ground up before eating. Chia seeds are another source of omega-3 fats that are currently quite popular and do not need to be ground up.

People who are vegetarian or vegan or simply do not want to eat fish can get adequate amounts of omega-3 from purely plant-based sources. Eating 1/4 to 1/2 cup of nuts and seeds per day along with a variety of vegetables to provide the nutrients needed to convert the precursor omega-3 to EPA and DHA works. Raw nuts are best because when omega-3 fats are exposed to heat, they start to break down. To ensure the conversion pathway is working optimally, it is also necessary for the person not to smoke or be exposed to heavy metals.

## Fish Oil Supplements

Even though fish oil supplements are not necessary if someone is eating a balanced, whole foods diet rich in nuts, seeds, vegetables, and fish, many people are not eating these foods and may choose to use fish oil supplements instead. Fish oil supplements can be an effective way of supplying the brain with these critical nutrients, but for a supplement to be beneficial, it has to be both effective and safe. This means it has to actually contain the EPA and DHA the consumer is seeking, and many do not. There are also source and quality-control issues with manufacturing fish oil that a consumer needs to understand in order to not waste their money and endanger their health.

## Quality

Because oceans are contaminated with heavy metals and pesticides, the fish that live in them are contaminated and can contain these toxins. Most people have heard of the dangers of mercury from eating fish, but this is only one of several toxins that can create problems. The amount of toxins in a fish depends on where it lived and how big the fish is, so it can vary quite dramatically. If a person is buying a fish oil supplement, it is critical that they buy a product free of toxins. The process by which these toxins are removed is called molecular distillation. If the label does not say that it has been molecularly distilled, the fish oil probably contains contaminants.

Fish oil must also be properly packaged and stored to maintain freshness. When fish oil is exposed to air, it starts to break-down and go rancid, a process that over time produces carcinogens. This process happens faster at higher temperatures, so fish oil should never be cooked with. Liquid fish oils need to be vacuum sealed when purchased, and after the bottle is open, it needs to be stored in the refrigerator or freezer. Softgels effectively vacuum seal the fish oil inside them, so they do not need to be kept in the refrigerator.

## How to Read the Label

The other issue with fish oil is understanding how to read the label. It can be very tricky for people who don't know exactly what they are looking for. First, check the serving size—the serving size is critical to accurately interpreting any label. The serving size on fish oil may be anywhere from one to six capsules. (Or one teaspoon to one tablespoon for liquid fish oil.) Fish oil labels usually state "total fish oil," and a typical amount is 1000mg per capsule. But there are lots of oils in fish other than EPA and DHA, so it is possible for a label to truthfully say "fish oil—1000mg per capsule" and still *not contain any EPA/DHA*. The critical value is the amount of EPA and DHA per serving (and again, check serving size!). Many fish oil labels do not state this information, and therefore contain no EPA and DHA.

EPA/DHA amounts cover a wide range. A common amount is 180mg of EPA in two capsules, which equals 90mg per capsule. If an adult wants to reach the therapeutic dose of 2000mg per day, that's 22 capsules per day! Higher potency fish oils will have 300 to 500mg of EPA per capsule, much easier to manage. The most potent capsules may potentially work out to be less expensive, even though the bottle may cost more. A $15 bottle of fish oil that requires someone to take 22 capsules per day for the therapeutic dose is going to run out quickly and end up being much more expensive than a $40 bottle of fish oil that requires four capsules per day.

To maintain healthy brain function, a person needs to consume 500 to 1000mg of EPA and 300 to 700mg of DHA per day. Children, up to the age of 10 to 12 (or about 100 pounds), are on the lower end. Adolescents are treated like adults and need the higher range.

## Contraindications

Fish oil supplements can cause problems if not used appropriately, so there are a few contraindications to be aware of. The most critical is that a person who is taking prescription blood thinning medication (Coumadin/Warfarin, Plavix) *must* avoid fish oil unless they have discussed it with their doctor *first*. Of course it is always a good idea for everybody to discuss any over the counter medications or vitamins with their doctor before starting them, but in this case it can be a life and death situation. Fish oil can change the therapeutic dose of the medication, and therefore, the doctor needs to be involved to adjust it if needed. Most surgeons require people to discontinue fish oil supplementation one week prior to surgery, but don't recommend that people stop eating fish.

Another, much more common problem with fish oil is digestion. Many people complain of digestive issues from fish oil, and those complaints are a big red flag of other problems, *not* just an uncomfortable nuisance or side effect to tolerate. If people complain of any kind of digestive issue from fish oil: nausea, diarrhea, upset stomach, or the most common, "repeating," which is fishy tasting burps, those symptoms indicate the person is not digesting the fish oil properly. If the person is not digesting fats and fish oil properly, they cannot benefit from it because nutrients have to be absorbed to work.

If someone complains of any of these issues, the first step is to find out if they are taking a high-quality fish oil. Meaning, does it meet all the criteria listed in the previous section? Lower-quality fish oils are much more likely to cause these problems. The second step is to ask when the person is taking the fish oil. Fats are best absorbed when there is other food in the stomach. Many people take pills at the end of the meal, but with fish oil, that creates a tendency for the fish oil to float on top, which decreases mixing with the digestive juices and sets the stage for fishy tasting burps. So the best time to take fish oil is at the beginning of the meal, which helps it mix with the rest of the food and gain maximum exposure to digestive juices.

Some people will still experience digestive issues, even when doing everything right. Many common digestive conditions such as irritable bowel syndrome (IBS) and gallbladder removal interfere with people's ability to digest and absorb fats. These people are even more likely to be suffering a deficiency of EPA and DHA as well as other essential fats because their ability to absorb fats is compromised. Even if they consume the right fats, either through food or through pills, they will still not benefit from them. These cases require a more comprehensive functional medicine approach to fix digestive function first. This requires referring the person to a doctor who practices functional medicine; most primary care physicians (PCP) and gastroenterologists will not take this comprehensive approach.

Taking fish oil supplements should wait until the person has a fully functioning digestive tract to save them from wasting time and money taking pills that are unlikely to benefit them. They need to first focus on restoring the full digestive function, so that when they eat the correct fats, they will get the full benefit. In these cases, adding fish oil supplements after they can digest them will accelerate progress.

Some fish oil supplements currently advertise themselves as "burpless." These fish oils have an enteric coating that prevents the capsule from breaking down in the stomach. This coating effectively prevents fishy tasting burps, but it also prevents the fish oil from being exposed to the digestive juices of the stomach, which makes it even harder for the body to absorb it! These fish oils are indeed better "tolerated," but are much less effective at the primary goal—getting EPA and DHA into the brain tissues that need it to properly respond to neurotransmitters.

# Your Brain Needs Fat: How to Feed Your Brain the Right Fats!

**Cook with olive oil and coconut oil**

Avoid vegetable oil, soy oil, corn oil, safflower oil. Canola oil can be used in baking, but be aware that most canola oil is genetically modified unless it is organic.

**Avoid hydrogenated fats (trans fats)**

Read food labels carefully. Where the label lists the different kinds of fats, "trans fat" should be 0 grams. If the words "hydrogenated" or "partially hydrogenated" are in the label, don't buy it. Restaurants often use hydrogenated fats—ask what oils are used, and choose restaurants that do not use any hydrogenated (trans) fats.

**Consume omega-3 fats**

Eat salmon, halibut, or mackerel two to three times per week (four to six ounce portions). You can also eat raw walnuts and pecans for a snack daily (a small handful).

**Are you deficient in EPA and DHA?**

1. Do you eat salmon or other fatty fish (halibut, mackerel, sardines, or herring) at least twice per week?
2. Do you eat walnuts, pecans, ground flax seeds, or chia seeds, along with several servings of vegetables most days?

Unless you answered yes to at least one of those questions, you are likely deficient in EPA and DHA and need to focus on getting these foods into your diet.

**How to get enough EPA and DHA**

1. Eat salmon, halibut, mackerel, sardines, or herring at least twice per week.
2. Eat 1/4 cup of raw walnuts or pecans per day—they make an easy, yummy snack.
3. Add ground flax seeds and/or chia seeds to salads, oatmeal, smoothies, and sauces.

# Protein: Tips to Enhance the Brain & Body

Chapter

# 9

Protein is constructed of amino acids. Digesting proteins is the process of breaking down the protein into amino acids, and then absorbing those amino acids into the blood stream where they will be used as the building blocks of the body: everything from muscle cells, DNA, and enzymes, to neurotransmitters. Most commonly, people think about eating protein to build muscle, but protein is also required for neurotransmitters. Without adequate protein, deficiencies in neurotransmitters will occur.

For example, one particular amino acid called tryptophan is the back bone of serotonin. Lack of serotonin or irregular serotonin production leads to mood disruptions. Without adequate tryptophan, the body cannot make serotonin. Another amino acid, tyrosine, is required for dopamine production. Dopamine is necessary for regulating impulse control, and deficient dopamine is associated with ADHD (and Parkinson's disease) while excess dopamine is associated with psychotic states.

But these are just two examples of the many amino acids that the human body needs. People need all of the amino acids to function. We get amino acids by eating protein. People do not need to look for sources of tryptophan or tyrosine specifically, even though every Thanksgiving we hear that turkey is a good source of tryptophan. People don't need to eat turkey to get tryptophan; there are many food sources of tryptophan. We need to eat a variety of protein sources to get *all* the amino acids.

## Which Foods Contain Protein?

The densest sources of protein are animals: beef, chicken, turkey, pork, fish, and eggs. These foods have the most protein per bite. Soybeans are the next richest source of protein and provide nearly as much as animal-based foods. Beans, nuts, and dairy also have significant protein, but much less per bite. Nuts and dairy have other nutrients in addition to protein and are part of a balanced, whole foods diet, but they should not be relied on as primary protein sources because doing so would require eating excess calories to get adequate protein.

This does not mean that people need to eat meat to get adequate protein. People who choose to follow a vegetarian or vegan diet can get perfectly adequate protein from eating a variety of beans, grains, tofu, and tempeh along with nuts and seeds. The richest grain sources of protein are whole spelt, kamut, teff, and sorghum. Quinoa and amaranth are technically seeds but cooked and eaten similar to grains, so most people think of them as grains and they are important sources of protein.

## How Much Protein is Enough?

Ideally, every meal should contain protein. Breakfast is the most important meal to have protein. Of course, breakfast is also the meal that is most likely to not contain protein, or be skipped entirely. Eating a breakfast that contains protein provides the raw materials needed to make the neurotransmitters necessary to regulate activities and respond to the stresses of the day. Eating protein with every meal ensures those raw materials continue to be available, so the body doesn't have to break down muscle tissue. Eating protein with every meal also helps balance blood sugar, which is also critical to optimal mental and emotional functioning. (More on blood sugar in Chapter 14.)

But how much protein is enough? Several diets that are currently popular advocate extremely large amounts of protein, but not everyone needs that much. Protein needs vary depending on activity levels, stress levels, health goals, and various health conditions. Of course, larger people simply need more. The different forms of recommendations for optimal protein, such as 10 to 35 percent of calories from protein or eating 0.8 to 1.2 mg/kg of body weight also offer a large range, which can be quite confusing when it comes to figuring out optimal amounts of protein.

If a person wants to deeply analyze their diet and individually optimize all the variables, working with a nutritionist is recommended. To simply ensure adequate protein intake for brain function and mental health, approximately 50 grams per day is the recommended target. Eating less than that does put the person at risk of compromised neurotransmitter production that could affect mood and mental functioning. Ideally that 50mg would be divided among at least three meals per day, yielding a target of 15 to 20 grams per meal.

But even absolute numbers don't give people a clear indication of what it means in terms of real food. The following list contains examples of a 15- to -20 gram serving of protein:

- 2 ounce portion of fish, chicken, or beef (half the size of your palm)
- 3 eggs
- 1/3 block of tofu
- 1 cup of beans
- 6 ounces of Greek yogurt or 12 ounces of regular yogurt, but watch the sugar (yogurt is loaded with huge amounts of sugar or chemical artificial sweeteners—if eating yogurt, eat *plain* yogurt)

Mixing and matching a variety of protein-containing foods will ensure that people eat adequate amounts of protein.

## The Controversy Over Soy

One form of protein that should not be eaten in large quantities is soy protein isolate. The extended controversy over whether soy is good or bad revolves mostly around the form of soy. Populations that consume soy as their dominant or even sole form of protein have repeatedly been shown to have lower rates of inflammatory diseases such as cardiovascular disease, cancer, and autoimmune disease (Nagata et al., 2014). However, other studies, many of them done in mice and rats, have correlated soy intake with higher levels of inflammation (D'Adamo & Sahin, 2014). This contradiction has spawned quite a lot of contradictory, and therefore confusing, recommendations about eating soy.

The issue that rarely gets addressed is that **the form of soy matters.** In the population studies, the form of soy eaten was the traditional forms: tofu, tempeh, and edamame. However, the dominant form of soy consumed in the U.S. is soy protein isolate. Soy protein isolate is part of the by-product that is left over after soy oil is extracted from soybeans. A significant fraction of that by-product is protein, which can be isolated from the other constituents and is therefore called "soy protein isolate."

Even though this substance is a pure protein, many people do not digest it well, which means they may not be getting the amino acids out of it. Poor digestion can trigger an inflammatory response, resulting in digestive symptoms such as gas, bloating, and constipation as well as more systemic inflammatory symptoms that manifest as other diseases. Soy protein isolate is the most common protein source used in protein bars, protein drinks, and vegetarian "sausages" (fake meat products). It is also added to many packaged foods to boost protein content.

## Question Digestion

While soy protein isolate can be particularly problematic to digest, all proteins require sufficient digestive power to break them down into amino acids. When that digestive function is lacking, it is possible for a person to suffer a deficiency in neurotransmitters due to inadequate amino acids despite the person consuming adequate amounts of dietary protein. People with IBS, colitis, and gastroesophageal reflux disease (GERD), which is reflux or chronic heartburn, are most at risk.

GERD poses a particular risk of nutrient deficiency because of the medications used to treat it. More and more research is coming to light showing the negative effects of using acid-reducing medication long-term (Wallerstedt, Fastbom, Linke, & Vitols, 2017). These medications are available both over the counter as well as by prescription, and all warn to not use them for more than six weeks. But many people do use these medications for much longer than that, extending to years and sometimes even decades.

However, this does not mean that people should immediately discontinue these medications. They first need to address the underlying causes of the symptoms that the medications are treating. Untreated GERD not only causes discomfort or pain, it also increases the risk of more advanced disease. Working with a functional medicine doctor will be necessary in most cases because most doctors will continue recommending the medication rather than fixing the underlying problem so that the medication is no longer needed. Many people are taking these medications long-term because their doctor advised them to, and they have never worked with a doctor who can help them address the underlying causes of the GERD and heal their digestive tract so they no longer need the medication.

# Tyrosine and Tryptophan

Because of their connection to neurotransmitters, tyrosine and tryptophan are available as over-the-counter supplements and advertised as helpful for mental health. But these amino acids are simply not necessary to take in supplement form when the diet contains adequate protein and digestive function is sufficient to break down that protein into amino acids. Supplemental tyrosine or tryptophan will only be helpful in the unusual situations where other medical conditions are interfering with diet or digestion.

One particularly difficult clinical situation where tyrosine can be helpful is in children who suffer ADHD, hyperactive type, where impulse control is the dominant symptom *and* who refuse to eat protein. Many children are picky eaters and, when kids with ADHD refuse to eat protein, it worsens the symptoms of ADHD, which often makes them even more picky about eating. This vicious cycle can be difficult to break. Using supplemental tyrosine, along with other appropriate therapies, can help break that vicious cycle.

Tryptophan, the amino acid that forms the backbone of serotonin, is also available as a supplement. Multiple biochemical transformations are required to turn tryptophan into serotonin, and the last step in that process before serotonin is 5-hydroxytryptophan, or 5-HTP. 5-HTP supports serotonin production much more effectively than tryptophan, and it is also available as a supplement. It is advertised as helpful for treating depression and anxiety and can be helpful in those situations. However, because it works on the same pathways as the selective serotonin reuptake inhibitor (SSRI) class of medications, 5-HTP should *never* be taken along with a full dose of SSRI. Adding 5-HTP when someone is already on a full dose of SSRI can lead to a serotonin syndrome, where the brain actually has too much serotonin. Like everything in medicine, too much is as problematic as not enough. If someone feels their SSRI medication is not effectively controlling their depression, warn them that just because a product is available over-the-counter, it can still interact with some medications.

One particular situation when 5-HTP can be particularly helpful is when people are suffering withdrawal symptoms from weaning off an SSRI. Withdrawal symptoms are not a return of symptoms that led to the SSRI being prescribed, it refers to the dizziness, disequilibrium, and electrical sensations that *some* people experience. Not everyone experiences these symptoms, but if such symptoms are interfering with a person's discontinuing an SSRI, using a small dose of 5-HTP (50 to 100mg) *after* discontinuing the SSRI will help the body adapt more quickly, lessening or even resolving the withdrawal symptoms.

# B-vitamins for Handling Stress

There are eight different B vitamins that constitute a complete "B-complex." Each is labeled by both a number and a name:

- B1 - Thiamine
- B2 - Riboflavin
- B3 - Niacin
- B5 - Pantothenic acid
- B6 - Pyridoxine
- B7 - Biotin
- B9 - Folic acid
- B12 - Cobalamin

Each of these vitamins plays many different roles in biochemical reactions throughout the body. The reason that B vitamins are critical for mental health is because they are required as co-factors in many of the reactions necessary to make neurotransmitters and hormones.

Remember how the amino acid tryptophan is required for serotonin production? For each of the steps that convert tryptophan to serotonin, other vitamins and minerals are necessary for the biochemical reaction to work. B1 (thiamin), B3 (niacin), B6 (pyridoxine), and B9 (folic acid) are all required just to make serotonin. Producing other neurotransmitters requires those as well as other B-vitamins, so an adequate supply of B-vitamins is critical to the body's ability to make neurotransmitters.

**Similarly, B-vitamins are necessary to handle stress appropriately.** The adrenal glands produce a variety of hormones and other signals to regulate multiple body and brain functions in order to maintain homeostasis, and B-vitamins are necessary to produce many of those signals. An inadequate supply of B-vitamins will compromise a person's ability to cope with stress.

The other side of B-vitamins being required to cope with stress is that higher stress increases demand for B-vitamins. The same person will need more B-vitamins to feel their best during high-stress times versus lower-stress times. And people are not all the same; some people require more B-vitamins than others to cope with the same level of stress.

The combination of high-stress lifestyles and poor eating puts Americans at particularly high risk for B-vitamin deficiency. While it may not be severe enough to cause a true deficiency disease, it can be severe enough to affect mental health and decrease ability to cope with stress. One easy way to give people the best chance to be resilient to stress is to ensure they have adequate B-vitamin intake for their situation and physiology.

## Best Food Sources of B-Vitamins

Eating a whole foods diet will give most people the B-vitamins they need. Many foods are sources of B-vitamins: whole grains, lentils, beans, bananas, tempeh, and nutritional yeast. The richest source of B-vitamins is whole grains, but many people have incorrect ideas about where to get whole grains because labels are so often designed to be misleading.

Eating a whole grain means the grain kernel is intact, it has not been pulverized into flour. When the grain is cooked and eaten in this form, the maximum amount of B-vitamins are available. Once the grain has been ground into flour, the B-vitamins start breaking down. However, not all flours are equal; some are much better than others. Some flours are made from the entire grain kernel, which includes the bran and the germ portions in addition to the endosperm. When flour is made this way, it is whole grain flour. Some flour is made by stripping off the bran and germ portions, and then making flour from just the remaining endosperm. This is known as refined flour, white flour, unbleached wheat flour, or just wheat flour. Because most of the fiber is in the bran, while most of the nutrients are in the germ, white flour is devoid of the nutrients. But it is still important not to confuse whole grain flour with the whole grain itself.

The best source of B-vitamins is whole grains. Below are pictures of whole grains. Familiar grains: corn, wheat, brown rice, wild rice.

Less familiar grains: millet, quinoa, oat groats.

The next best sources of B-vitamins after true whole grains are products made with whole grain flour. Whole grain bread, whole grain pasta, and whole grain crackers all have big advantages over those same products made with refined flour because they still contain some B-vitamins and fiber, but it is important to not confuse whole grain flour with the whole grain itself. The B-vitamins and fiber have not been stripped out from whole grain flours.

The tricky part is figuring out which breads, pastas, and crackers are actually made from whole grain flour. Labels are designed to be misleading, often claiming there are whole grains in the product when there are no actual whole grains at all. See the following example of a product label: The front label claims it has eight grams of whole grains. But by reading the actual ingredient label, the first two ingredients are shown to be refined flour, and a whole grain flour isn't listed until the third item. Then toward the very end, which means there is a very small amount, other grains are listed without specifying what form they are in.

---

# 8 Whole Grains Bread Ingredients

Enriched Wheat Flour (Flour, Malted Barley Flour, Reduced Iron, Niacin, Thiamin Mononitrate (Vitamin B1) Riboflavin (Vitamin B2) Folic Acid), Water, **Whole Wheat Flour**, Wheat Gluten, Honey, Sunflower Seeds, Sugar, Yeast, Bulgur Wheat, Soybean Oil, Wheat Brain, Salt, Crushed Wheat, Molasses, Rye Flakes, Barley, Oat Flakes, Triticale, Millet, Corn Grits, Calcium Propionate (Preservative), Flaxseed, Datem, Monoglycerides, Buckwheat, Rice Flour, Calcium Sulfate, Grain Vinegar, Soy Lecithin, Citric Acid, Potassium Iodate

---

The key to reading labels wisely is looking for the word "whole" first. **The first ingredient should be "whole wheat flour" or "whole oat flour."** The type of flour is not the important part; the critical point is that the first word is "whole." If it says wheat flour, enriched wheat flour, multi-grain flour, or durum semolina, these are all synonymous with refined white flour.

Other words are used that can be misleading. Organic flour does not mean it's a whole grain flour. Whole grain flour may or may not be organic, and white flour may or may not be organic. "Multi-grain" is another term that is used to imply healthier, but again, unless the multiple flours are all whole grain flours, they are still refined.

Another misconception many people have is that if the bread is brown, it is made with whole grain. While bread made with whole wheat flour is typically brown, not all brown breads contain whole wheat flour. The reason for the color difference between these loaves of bread is not the presence of whole wheat flour but molasses. Molasses makes the bread brown. In the bottom box, whole wheat flour is at least the third ingredient, so there is some, but that is not always true.

---

# White Bread Ingredients

Enriched Wheat Flour (Wheat Flour, Malted Barley Flour, Niacin, Iron, Thiamin Mononitrate, Riboflavin, Folic Acid), Water, High Fructose Corn Syrup, Yeast, Wheat Gluten, Contains 2% Or Less Of The Following: Soybean Oil, Honey, Salt, Dough Conditioners (Sodium Stearoyl Lactylate, Monoglycerides, Calcium Peroxide, Ascorbic Acid), Calcium Propionate (Preservative), Yeast Nutrients (Calcium Sulfate, Ammonium Sulfate, Ammonium Chloride), Soy Lecithin.

---

# Wheat Bread Ingredients

Enriched Wheat Flour (Wheat Flour, Barley Malt, Niacin, Iron, Thiamin Mononitrate, Riboflavin, Folic Acid), Water, Whole Wheat Flour, High Fructose Corn Syrup, Yeast, Wheat Bran, Contains 2% or Less of The Following: Honey, Molasses, Soybean Oil, Salt, Dough Conditioners (Mono-and Diglyercrides, Ethoyxlated Mono-Anddiglycerides, Sodium Stearoyl Lactylate, Calcium Peroxide), Sugar, Corn Flour, Yeast Nutrients (Monocalcium Phosphate, Ammonium Sulfate, Calcium Sulfate), Calcium Propioniate (Preservative), Soy Lecithin

Below is a sample label of true whole wheat bread, where whole wheat flour is the first ingredient and no white flour is used. The front label may not look all that different from the others shown, which is why it is critical to always read ingredient lists.

---

# Whole Wheat Bread Ingredients

**Whole wheat flour**, water, wheat berries, wheat gluten, sugar, yeast, unsulphured molasses, soybean oil, contains 2 percent or less of: wheat, sugarcane fiber, salt, calcium propionate and sorbic acid to retard spoilage, distilled monoglycerides, datem (dough conditioner), whey (milk), soy lecithin.

---

## B-vitamin Insufficiency

Most people do get the recommended dietary allowance (RDA) of B-vitamins, which does prevent true deficiency diseases. But many people do not eat enough B-vitamins to function at their best, and instead experience a state of chronic insufficiency. There are two main contributing factors to B-vitamin insufficiency:

1. Eating a processed food diet that lacks foods which contain B-vitamins
2. Stress

Stress increases the body's demand for B-vitamins. An individual will need more B-vitamins to function optimally under stressful conditions compared to ideal conditions. The flip side of this relationship is that when a person does not eat adequate B-vitamins, it compromises their ability to cope with stress. Therefore the combination of nutrition-depleted diets with high-stress lifestyles leaves many people vulnerable to suffering the effects of B-vitamin insufficiency. Again, insufficient B-vitamins interferes with neurotransmitter production and ability to cope with stress, which both directly and indirectly can contribute to several forms of depression and other mental illness.

Correcting B-vitamin insufficiency is yet another reason to eat a whole foods diet rich in vegetables and whole grains and avoid processed food. Working with diet will always be necessary, but often difficult, for people who are feeling stressed. Particularly when the stress leads to depression, lack of motivation can be a particularly big obstacle. While it is never the full answer, using a B-complex supplement can help in these situations.

The only B-vitamin that has a laboratory test that is clinically useful for detecting insufficiency is B12, which will be discussed separately in the next section. But B-vitamin insufficiency can be assessed clinically, by analyzing diet, stress level, and mental health. The combination of a nutrient-poor diet, high stress, fatigue, and depression indicate a strong possibility of B-vitamin insufficiency contributing to the symptoms. If someone is under a lot of stress, but feeling more anxious or high-strung because of it, rather than tired and depressed, it is unlikely that B-vitamin insufficiency is a contributing factor in those cases.

# B-Complex Supplements

The best test of whether there is truly a B-vitamin insufficiency is to try a B-complex challenge. People respond quickly when B-vitamins are the nutrients they are missing. It may be dramatic, or it may be more subtle, but people notice improved energy and mood within days to weeks of starting a B-complex supplement if that is what is needed.

Looking at the B-vitamin section of a pharmacy can be completely overwhelming. B-vitamins are available individually, as well as in a variety of combinations and potencies. The safest way to do a challenge test with B-vitamins is to use a B-complex in a B-50 potency. A B-50 potency means the supplement contains 50mg of B1, 50mg of B2, 50mg of B3, and 50mg of B6. The other B-vitamins will be in different amounts. Below is a sample of the back label, the nutrition information, of a B-50. The front label may say B-50, but may say B-complex, Stress-B, or something else entirely.

## Supplement Facts

Serving Size: 1 capsule
Servings Per Container: 250

| Ingredient | Amount | % Daily Value |
|---|---|---|
| Thiamin (Vitamin B-1) | 50mg | 3333 |
| Riboflavin (Vitamin B-2) | 50mg | 2941 |
| Ciacin (Citamin B-3) | 50mg | 250 |
| Vitamin B-6 (From Pyridoxine HCl) | 50mg | 2500 |
| Folic Acid | 400mcg | 100 |
| Vitamin B-12 (as Cyanocobalamin) | 50mg | 833 |
| Biotin | 50mg | 17 |
| Pantothenic Acid (from Calcium Pantothenate) | 40mg | 400 |
| PABA | 50mg | + |
| Choline | 50mg | + |
| Inositol | 50mg | + |

While taking a B-complex is much safer than taking high doses of one individual B-vitamin, there are still a few issues to be aware of. B-vitamins can cause nausea or upset stomach in many people. Taking it with food will prevent this issue in the vast majority of situations. Some people do find they need to eat a full meal with a B-complex to tolerate it comfortably.

There is also the possibility of a niacin flush. Niacin flush reactions are predictable at high doses of niacin, but extremely rare at the low dose found in a B-50. Even if someone has tried high-dose niacin and suffered niacin flush reactions, taking a B-50 is likely tolerable. If someone does have a niacin flush, they often think they are having an allergic reaction because their skin turns red and feels hot and itchy. This harmless, temporary reaction lasts a few minutes to an hour, and then completely resolves. Taking B-vitamins with food will also decrease the possibility of it and prevent it in some people who are sensitive to it.

Every once in a while, B-vitamins can provide too much of a good thing. When people experience a big improvement in energy when they take B-vitamins, occasionally they find that if they take them too late in the day, they can interfere with sleep. Most people are not that sensitive, but always start B-complex in the morning.

**CASE STUDY**

# B-vitamins and Depression

One particularly dramatic case of just how powerful B-complex can be is the case of a 43-year-old social worker. She had first been hospitalized for depression after a suicide attempt as a teenager. Despite being on medications ever since, she described her life as, "Forcing myself to meet my responsibilities, which I do for the sake of my children." She was stable when she sought the help of functional medicine, but hoping she could feel much better than she did.

At her first visit, I ordered many tests, but a basic dietary review showed that her diet was quite depleted in B-vitamin-containing foods. Also, she was under a lot of family and financial stress, which certainly contributed to her depression, though it was clear that her depression was also contributing to both the family and financial stress.

In addition, her long history of clinical depression, as well as family history of depression, pointed toward a possibility that she may be in the minority of people who simply need more than the RDA of B-vitamins to function at their best, even under non-stressful conditions. For all of these reasons, I started her on a B-50 at the very first visit.

Before her lab results came in, she called me and said, "Is this what normal people feel like?" She described feeling joy, reportedly for the first time in her life, just from sharing a moment of simple fun while playing with one of her children. Such moments had happened often, but never before had she experienced happiness from them.

Life-long clinical depression is never cured in one moment, and other physical and psychological treatments were still necessary for her to reach optimum health. But B-complex was a breakthrough treatment that not only helped her feel better directly, but also helped other therapies that were already in place work more effectively. She improved so much that she questioned if she still needed her medication. After weaning off the medication, she discovered she actually felt better off medication than on medication. She also learned to eat the foods needed to supply all the nutrients to feel her best, and found that she didn't need to rely on the B-complex pill.

Over the next several years, we discovered that during times of more intense stress, her depression could start to creep back in, and taking B-complex supported her ability to cope with stress and not slip back into old emotional patterns. Whether this is because stress could also cause her diet to slip back into old patterns and she would stop eating the B-vitamins she needed, or if stress increased her body's demand for B-vitamins beyond what she could obtain through diet was never clearly determined, but both scenarios happen and B-complex provides critical support for some people.

# Taking the Complexity Out of B-complex

Eight different B-vitamins make up what is commonly referred to as "B-complex." B-vitamins are critical to mental health because they are co-factors in producing neurotransmitters and hormones. Lacking any of the B-vitamins compromises your ability to handle stress and leaves you feeling moody, depressed, anxious, irritable, and exhausted. Below are the B-vitamins:

B1 - Thiamin
B2 - Riboflavin
B3 - Niacin
B5 - Pantothenic acid
B6 - Pyridoxine
B7 - Biotin
B9 - Folic acid
B12 - Cobalamin

**Do you need more B-vitamins?**
To determine if you may benefit from an increased intake of B-vitamins, take the following quiz:

1. Are you currently under a lot of stress?_____

2. Have you been under a lot of stress for more than six months?_____

3. Do you feel tired often? _____

4. Do you feel that no matter how much sleep you get, you're still tired? _____

5. Do you need coffee to "get going" in the morning? _____

6. Do you feel so stressed out that sometimes you just don't care anymore? _____

7. Are you depressed? _____

*Score:* Tally up the number of "yes" responses to see which category you fit in below.

> 0-2: Low probability of benefiting from increased intake of B-vitamins
>
> 3-5: Medium probability of benefiting from increased intake of B-vitamins
>
> 6-7: High probability of benefiting from increased intake of B-vitamins

**Tips for taking B-complex**

1. Take B-complex in the morning to give you an energy boost.
2. Take B-complex with food to prevent any upset stomach.

You will notice a difference within days to weeks in both energy and mood if B-complex is a missing link for you.

# B12 and Folic Acid for Anxiety, Depression and Fatigue

B12 is one individual B-vitamin and is included in the B-complex discussed in the previous chapter. However, B12 requires extra attention as an individual vitamin because of its powerful relationship with mental health. Even though doctors have known for generations that B12 deficiency causes depression, it still goes undiagnosed much too often. Many people need B12 treatment that requires forms of B12 other than what is available in food or a B-complex supplement.

The most common reason for B12 deficiency is a disease called pernicious anemia. Pernicious anemia is a hereditary autoimmune condition that destroys the parietal cells of the stomach. The parietal cells secrete intrinsic factor, which is required for absorbing B12. Without intrinsic factor, B12 is not absorbed, and the person develops a B12 deficiency.

Pernicious anemia develops slowly over many years, so symptoms onset insidiously and slowly worsen over time. Typical onset starts in middle age or the elderly years, but more and more often younger people are requiring B12 therapy. One theory for this change is that the highly-inflammatory diets most Americans eat may be triggering the autoimmune process earlier and accelerating its progression. While B12 deficiency certainly becomes more common in an older population, it should still be considered as a possible etiology even in younger people.

Other reasons to evaluate B12 status in people of all ages are any kind of digestive dysfunction. Some gastrointestinal diseases diminish the ability to absorb B12, and if someone has both digestive problems and depression, B12 should be measured. The most rapidly-growing cause of B12 deficiency is gastric bypass surgery. All people with gastric bypass will need B12 treatment.

The only dietary cause of B12 deficiency is veganism. B12 is present in animal products, so if someone is strictly avoiding all animal-based foods, a B12 deficiency will result. Being healthy on a vegan diet requires either eating a special form of nutritional yeast that has had B12 added, or supplementing with B12. In this case, the amount of B12 in a B-complex is perfectly sufficient because absorption is not an issue. People do not need to eat large amounts of animal products to get all the B12 they need; small amounts are sufficient. People who have "vegetarian tendencies," meaning they typically avoid animals but occasionally consume eggs, dairy, or fish will get all the B12 they need (as long as they can absorb it).

## Symptoms of B12 Deficiency

The primary symptoms of B12 deficiency are fatigue and depression. Sometimes one will precede the other, but typically they develop together. Without treatment they will progress, slowly, and eventually other symptoms will develop. Neuropathy and anemia are the next stages, and if left untreated for a long period of time, B12 deficiency can cause dementia. (Unless someone has not received any medical care, B12 deficiency dementia is a rare cause of dementia in the United States currently.)

In any case of progressive, non-transient depression, B12 should be evaluated. When B12 deficiency is the cause of someone's depression, it is the only treatment that will truly help. Anti-depressant medications may help temporarily, but since they aren't treating the true underlying cause, the effects tend to diminish as the disease continues to progress.

## Assessing for B12 Deficiency

Testing for B12 is a simple blood test that can be done by any doctor. It is not typically part of the labs done at a screening physical, so do not assume that it has already been tested. Doctors only test for B12 when there is reason to suspect B12 deficiency. Because pernicious anemia typically onsets later in life, during the elderly or middle-age years, younger people are often not tested for B12 deficiency. But more and more often, pernicious anemia is onsetting at younger ages, so even younger people should be tested when they are exhibiting symptoms that could be due to B12 deficiency.

When someone gets his/her B12 tested, they should always ask for the result. Sometimes doctors will simply inform the patient that, "your labs are normal." With B12, the result needs to be interpreted correctly because even many people who are in the low normal range can already be suffering the effects of B12 deficiency.

The normal range of B12 is typically 200 to 1100pg/mL, with some small variations depending on the lab. But substantial data (Devalia, Hamilton, Molloy, & British Committee for Standards in Haematology, 2014) shows that significant numbers of people in the 200 to 400pg/mL range who are exhibiting symptoms of B12 deficiency will respond to B12 therapy. In this range, clinical symptoms indicate treatment, and the person should work with his/her doctor to determine the best treatment.

B12 treatment can be either oral or an intramuscular injection. If high-dose sublingual B12 is effective, typically that is the preferable option. However, many people respond only to injections. Dosing and frequency is individualized based on response and lab work results, but the most common schedule for injections is once per month.

## Folic Acid/L-5-MTHF

Folic acid is another B-vitamin that deserves its own special attention because of its connection with mental health. Folic acid is required for making serotonin, dopamine, and norepinephrine, so folic acid deficiency will cause many complex issues with neurotransmitters. How much folic acid is enough is currently a subject of intense debate because research in different areas of medicine conflict: Some show higher levels improve health, some show that higher levels might be dangerous.

In the world of psychiatry, one piece of the puzzle is beginning to emerge. Mutations in the MTHFR gene cause a decreased ability to turn folic acid into its active form L-5-methytetrahyrofolate (L-5-MTHF). Therefore, people who have this gene mutation can eat sufficient folic acid, test normal for folic acid, and still suffer the mood consequences of folic acid deficiency because they lack sufficient L-5-MTHF.

The full medical implications of these gene mutations are still not fully understood, but as research develops it will become more clear who needs to be tested for this mutation and what the optimal treatment is for those who have it. In the realm of mental health, there is significant evidence that people with this mutation can benefit from 5-MTHF supplementation (also marketed as the prescription drug Deplin).

When people have persistent and progressive issues with depression, anxiety, and fatigue, despite treatment, or have multiple complicated mental health diagnoses, ask if their psychiatrist has done MTHFR testing. Taking 5-MTHF in large doses by people who do not need it has not been shown to be safe, and may even put people at risk, so caution people that testing and working with a prescriber is the only safe approach.

## CASE STUDY
# Vitamins D and B12

Kristen came to me saying she *really* didn't want to start medication. But she had been working with a therapist for over two years and, despite that, she felt life was becoming more and more of a struggle. She even said she was probably depressed, even though she didn't want to admit it. She diligently exercised every day, ate a whole foods diet, and avoided foods with chemicals in them. She was also trying to meditate more often.

Despite all of that, in the past year, she was having more episodes of "wondering" what it would be like if a terrible accident happened to her, and she was disturbed that such thoughts did not upset her and, at bad times, even felt like a relief. Her therapist had suggested that she might have a neurochemical imbalance, which was impeding their work, and had suggested seeing a psychiatrist as well. She had done that and been prescribed Effexor, but she still wanted to see if something else could work before resorting to medications.

At that first visit, I did basic lab work because it had been over a year since she had seen her PCP. The lab work included thyroid, vitamin D, vitamin B12, and MTHFR testing. Her thyroid was normal, but her vitamin D and vitamin B12 were both at the low end of the normal range. She also had two copies of the MTHFR gene mutation. Based on her numbers, I gave her vitamin D 2000IU per day, sublingual B12 5000mcg per day, and 5-MTHF 3mg per day.

One month later, she said, "I've had a good month." She'd had good months, even good seasons before, and she said she often felt better in the spring. Her spring improvement hadn't happened the last few years, but this year it did. Even though she often felt better in spring, it also brought extra stress with the end of the school year at her job as a high school teacher. Because of that extra stress, and to help her body respond more quickly to the nutrients, I added some adrenal support in the form of licorice.

Another month later, she said she felt even more improvement, that her mood was better and more stable than it had been in a few years, even during summer. She was still tired after work and still sometimes got anxious and down about stress at work, but she was more motivated to do fun things on the weekend and didn't feel quite so beaten down by work. She said even her husband had commented that she seemed happier, a little more like how she used to be.

We decided to continue the adrenal support until school finished in June, and then see if she felt good in summer without it. We also decided to continue the doses of B12 and D required to keep her at the high end of normal instead of the low end for at least a year to prevent any seasonal variations while we evaluated if she had truly reached optimal health.

Over the summer, she said she felt better than she had in years, and when school started again in the fall she had a renewed enthusiasm for, and enjoyment of, her job. Despite the usual stresses, her increased resilience continued through the winter and the next spring. She told me, "In therapy I was even able to finally work out some issues with my husband that I simply hadn't been able to in the previous years."

Kristen will continue to need to have vitamins D and B12 monitored on a yearly basis to make sure she is staying at the right levels to prevent any return of symptoms. We lowered the 5-MTHF dose to 1mg as maintenance, and she continued to do well.

# Vitamin D for Depression and Seasonal Affective Disorder

Vitamin D comes in two forms: ergocalciferol (vitamin D2) and cholecalciferol (vitamin D3). D3 is the form that the human body uses. The deficiency disease that results from severe vitamin D deficiency is called osteomalacia (in kids, rickets), which results in softening of the bone. This disease is quite rare in the U.S. at this point, but there is substantial research that shows that suboptimal levels of vitamin D are correlated with higher rates of depression, seasonal affective disorder (SAD), osteoporosis, cancer, arthritis, and cardiovascular disease (Vasquez, Manso, & Cannell, 2004). Not all of these diseases have been shown to respond to raising vitamin D levels, which has led to some controversy about the true cause and effect relationship between vitamin D and health. However, there are studies which show that treating people who suffer from depression or SAD improves symptoms (Shaffer et al., 2014).

Vitamin D has one dramatic and curious difference from most other nutrients—there are almost no natural food sources of vitamin D. (Certain foods, like milk, are now typically fortified with vitamin D in the U.S.) Vitamin D is actually produced in the body, by certain cells in the skin called keratinocytes when they are exposed to sunlight (or other sources of ultraviolet light).

The most "natural" way to increase vitamin D levels is by increasing exposure to sunlight. However, excessive exposure to sunlight carries the well-known effects of increased skin aging and increased risk of skin cancer. While being outside with moderate exposure to sunlight is beneficial to health, care must still be taken to avoid over-exposure or sunburn. It is also important to note that wearing sunscreen blocks vitamin D production.

Because of these risks, and because most people in the modern world spend much more time indoors than humans have through most of history, vitamin D supplementation is often necessary. The RDA for vitamin D supplementation is 600IU per day, but controversy still swirls around this recommendation. Realistically, it is impossible to make a one-size-fits-all recommendation because there are so many variables that affect how much vitamin D a person is making. How much vitamin D a person makes depends on how much sun exposure he/she gets and how intense the UV light is: latitude and time of day both factor in dramatically. Sunlight at noon is much stronger than at 5 pm. In the northern hemisphere, sunlight in the summer is more intense than in the winter, and sun intensity is always greater in Arizona than in Alaska, year-round. Skin color also influences the amount of vitamin D produced, even with equal intensity of sunlight.

**Because of all these variables, making a one-size-fits-all recommendation for vitamin D supplementation, or even sunlight exposure, simply does not make sense.** Even the commonly-professed "natural" recommendation that "all people should get 15 minutes of sunlight on their faces every day to make vitamin D" does not take into account all those important variables. Therefore, the best approach is to treat each person as a unique individual, test vitamin D, and treat accordingly.

When this approach is taken, the problem of vitamin D toxicity is avoided. Vitamin D toxicity causes hypercalcemia, which can damage many different tissues and organs. But vitamin D toxicity is easily avoided as long as appropriate monitoring of vitamin D levels continues. People should not take vitamin D long-term without periodic monitoring (every one to three years, or sooner if there are any changes in health). Many primary care physicians now test vitamin D, but some do not. Patients should not only ask if their vitamin D has been checked, but they also should ask what the number is. The normal range is typically 30 to 100ng/mL, but the optimal range is 45 to 65ng/mL (Vasquez et al., 2004). Patients should not assume that if they are told they are "normal" that they are in the optimal range. People in the low normal range can benefit from increasing vitamin D into the optimal range.

Response to vitamin D therapy is unlikely to be as dramatic as that of some people to B-vitamin therapy. Very rarely do people notice a difference within the first few weeks of taking it. (When that happens, usually the person had extremely low vitamin D.) More typically, symptoms improve and stabilize more subtlety, over several months. However, optimal vitamin D levels are still a critical foundation to healthy mood and to healthy immune function as well.

# Magnesium and Calcium: Minerals for the Body and Mind

Chapter

# 13

Magnesium is a mineral, and along with many other minerals, it plays many roles in the body. Magnesium deficiency is one of the most common nutritional causes of mental health problems. The role of magnesium is going to be the primary focus of this section, but it is impossible to thoroughly discuss magnesium without also discussing calcium because they must be in balance with each other for the nervous system to function properly.

Magnesium is required for relaxation. Without adequate magnesium, nerve cells cannot relax, leading to hypersensitivity that can manifest as anxiety, irritability, ADHD, bipolar, and increased sensitivity to pain. Magnesium is also necessary for muscle cells to relax, so magnesium deficiency leads to muscle tension and the many pain syndromes associated with muscular dysfunction: restless legs, muscle cramps, headaches, migraines, fibromyalgia, and some forms of back pain and sciatica.

The tricky part of evaluating magnesium is that there is no clinically-useful laboratory test to measure it. Serum magnesium can be tested, but it is only an accurate indication of the serum levels—*not* the levels in the rest of the body. Because the body will steal magnesium from the muscles, brain, and bones to keep serum magnesium normal, magnesium levels have to drop to dangerously-low levels in those tissues before the deficiency will show up on a serum magnesium test. **People will suffer many painful symptoms of magnesium deficiency long before it will show up on a serum magnesium test, so the best way to look for deficiency is by clinical evaluation of symptoms.**

No single symptom definitively indicates magnesium deficiency, but many symptoms indicate the possibility of it. Magnesium deficiency should be considered as a potential cause any time any of the symptoms on the following lists are encountered. All of these symptoms have more than one possible cause, and usually more than one factor is contributing to a person's symptoms by the time they reach the doctor. But if a person has several of these symptoms, there is a very high probability that magnesium deficiency is contributing to many or all of them.

**Mental/emotional symptoms that indicate possible magnesium deficiency:**

- Anxiety
- Panic attacks
- Irritability
- Short temper/excessive anger

- Difficulty focusing
- Heightened sensitivity to pain

**Physical symptoms that indicate possible magnesium deficiency:**

- Poor sleep
- Restless leg syndrome
- Frequent muscle cramps (typically at night or while exercising)
- Muscles twitches
- Menstrual cramps
- Headaches
- Migraines
- Fibromyalgia
- Constipation
- High blood pressure
- Heart palpitations

Magnesium deficiency is extremely common, and massively underestimated because of the fact that serum magnesium is not an accurate measure of total body magnesium (Ismail, Ismail, & Ismail, 2017). Magnesium deficiency has to be severe before it shows up on serum magnesium tests, but less severe magnesium deficiency can still cause substantial pain and distress, even before it reaches levels that are detectable on blood tests. Because it affects such a large portion of the population, routinely evaluating for magnesium deficiency *by clinical assessment* will benefit a huge number of people. The handout on page 114 includes patient information on magnesium as well as a self-assessment.

## Causes of Magnesium Deficiency

There are three distinct reasons for magnesium deficiency. For most people, more than one of them are contributing, and all need to be addressed.

### 1. Diet

The standard American processed food diet contains very little magnesium. Most people eat far too much refined flour and fat, which doesn't contain magnesium, and not enough vegetables, beans, and legumes, which are the best sources of magnesium. Other significant sources of magnesium that contribute in multiple ways to overall nutrition are nuts and whole grains. (See B-complex section of Chapter 10 for a full description of what a whole grain really is and how to not be fooled by deceptive advertising.)

### 2. Food contains less magnesium than in the past

Modern farming practices replace many of the nutrients in soil through the use of fertilizer. Typically, magnesium is not replaced in standard farming. When soil is farmed year after year, decade after decade, generation after generation, the magnesium levels drop and the plants growing in the soil do not contain as much magnesium as in the past (Guo, Nazim, Liang, & Yang, 2016).

### 3. Calcium excess

When people take large amounts of a single nutrient, they put themselves at risk of disrupting the balance of other nutrients. Sometimes large amounts of a single nutrient are necessary to correct a deficiency, but it is always critical to assess and manage the dose relative to other nutrients. The balance between magnesium and calcium is just one of many of these relationships, but it is one of the most common imbalances that causes health problems. Many people are taking calcium supplements without taking adequate magnesium and other minerals, and one of the first problems to arise is magnesium deficiency. The next section will talk about the role of calcium and how to keep it in balance with magnesium.

### 4. Stress and activity

Activity and stress both increase the body's demand for magnesium. Activity is critical to life and mental health, and Chapter 6 explains those benefits in detail. The key is to ensure a person's magnesium intake meets their needs based on personal activity level. Stress can be either positive or negative, but either way it needs to be accounted for when determining optimal magnesium intake.

## Correcting Magnesium Deficiency

The best way to get all nutrients is from food. The best food sources of magnesium are dark, leafy green vegetables—kale, chard, collard greens, spinach, mustard greens, beet greens and others. Other green vegetables are also excellent sources of magnesium, as are beans and legumes, nuts, and whole grains. All of these foods should be eaten on a daily basis as part of a healthy, balanced diet that gives the brain all the nutrients it needs to function at its best.

When people are severely deficient in magnesium and suffering symptoms because of it, replacing magnesium quickly through the use of supplements can speed recovery and help people experience just how important nutrients are. The RDA of magnesium is 300 to 400mg per day, but some people will need more than the RDA, at least temporarily, to fully recover from magnesium deficiency.

The most important warning about magnesium supplementation is that magnesium can cause osmotic diarrhea, which is more likely when it is poorly absorbed. People who suffer colitis, IBS, or other digestive problems that interfere with nutrient absorption are more at risk of this effect and are also more at risk of magnesium deficiency.

For these people, using the most absorbable form, magnesium glycinate, is recommended. Some people with more severe digestive problems may need to use topical forms of magnesium if their digestive tract is too inflamed to absorb nutrients. Topical magnesium creams or gels are also great for kids who can't swallow pills and may not like the taste of liquid magnesium. Epsom salt baths are another pleasurable way to absorb magnesium, for both kids and adults.

Kids are just as prone to magnesium deficiency as adults are, and magnesium deficiency in kids is just as common as it is in adults.

Magnesium comes in many forms, and magnesium glycinate is the most absorbable. The less absorbable forms, such as magnesium oxide, are typically easier to find and cheaper. Many people respond very well to any form, though they may need higher amounts if using magnesium oxide. The bottom line is always, "What works?" If someone's symptoms resolve, the form does not matter. If someone has symptoms of magnesium deficiency but supplementation does not give full relief or upsets the bowels, then the more absorbable forms should be tried.

## Balancing Magnesium and Calcium

Most people are much more aware of the importance of calcium than magnesium. Indeed, calcium is critical for health, and not just strong bones. (Magnesium is also important for strong bones.) But this emphasis on calcium has led to a damaging myth that now persists. When people hear repeatedly that calcium is good, they often start to think, "More calcium is better." This is simply not true—too much calcium actually can cause problems. The most common of these is magnesium deficiency.

The RDA of calcium is 1000 to 1200mg per day. But all too often this guideline gets stated as "Take 1200mg of calcium per day," which then gets interpreted as "take pills." But the RDA is a recommendation for total calcium consumption, and many people are eating significant amounts of calcium. If the person then adds 1200mg more of calcium on top of that, without eating or taking adequate magnesium, the imbalance will result in magnesium deficiency. Because so many people are taking calcium supplements, this is a very common problem.

Some food sources of calcium are also great sources of magnesium, and therefore are the best for keeping these key nutrients in balance. Leafy greens, an excellent source of magnesium, are also rich sources of calcium. Chard, collards, kale, mustard greens, beet greens, and spinach are all excellent sources of both magnesium and calcium, along with other green vegetables. Other major sources of calcium are dairy products, tofu, and tempeh.

When evaluating calcium consumption, it's important to note that many people, particularly middle-aged women and the elderly, are taking calcium supplements. Another source of calcium that people frequently overlook is antacids. Tums, and all the Tums generics, are 600mg of calcium. Just two per day put people at the RDA of calcium, even if they do not eat any other calcium. Going over the RDA once in a while will not cause any problems, but many people take Tums every day, sometimes multiple times per day. Taking two Tums, two to three times per day, on a regular basis will lead to the problems of calcium excess and magnesium deficiency.

Many people can benefit from supplementing calcium, and many people have been told by their doctor to take 1200mg of calcium per day. The critical evaluation that is so often not done is, "How much calcium is the person eating, and therefore, how much is coming from food and how much needs to be supplemented by this particular individual?" If the person does need calcium supplements, the other minerals *also* need to be supplemented to keep all the minerals in balance and prevent calcium excess from causing other deficiencies.

## CASE STUDY
# Calcium and Magnesium

Maria is a 64-year-old woman who came to my office one day complaining of severe headaches and constipation. She had headaches every day, typically waking up with it, and if she didn't wake up with a headache, she had one by mid-day. Years ago she had seen a doctor for the headaches, and she said the drug she tried made it worse, so she stopped taking it, didn't go back, and swore off doctors. More recently, her constipation, which had been a minor issue for a long time, was getting worse—she now needed to give herself an enema every day.

Despite these issues, the real reason she came to my office was because her daughter had twisted her arm into coming. Her daughter was a patient and was really worried about her mother. Over the past few years her mother had stopped traveling, and more recently, had stopped visiting local friends. When she visited her mother at her mother's home, she said her mother had developed many rigid behaviors that were bordering on ritualistic and she was worried her mother was developing obsessive-compulsive disorder (OCD).

Maria didn't complain of any kind of obsessive thoughts and acknowledged that she didn't travel as much anymore, but she blamed that simply on "getting older." It was not at all clear whether she had some unrecognized anxiety or OCD that was causing some of her physical symptoms, or if her behavior changes were simply due to the pain she was in.

While I was taking her medical history trying to figure out what was causing what and where all this started, she told me that about a decade earlier, shortly after she went through menopause, she was told she had "severe osteoporosis," and that she should take 1200mg of calcium every day. Being health conscious and proactive, she had diligently followed this instruction, along with increasing her dairy consumption because she "knew it was good for her bones." This is when I realized magnesium deficiency was likely a key factor in many of her symptoms because she was consuming an excessive amount of calcium and minimal amounts of magnesium.

At that point, I would have liked to have stopped her supplementation of calcium entirely, temporarily, to help her body regain balance as fast as possible, but she was too scared. Like so many women, she was completely convinced that calcium was the only way to treat osteoporosis, and that more calcium is better, even though calcium is only one aspect of treating osteoporosis, and that weight-bearing exercise is actually more effective.

We talked a lot about the role of calcium and the other minerals as well as how to balance them in the diet, and I was able to convince her to lower her calcium supplementation to 200mg per day. Because she was still taking calcium, and because the constipation was so severe, I started her on a higher dose of magnesium than I would typically start with, at 500mg. 500mg is not actually a high dose; many people need 500mg (sometimes even more), but 500mg is enough to disrupt bowel function in some people, so typically I would start lower and increase gradually.

One month later she returned to the office saying that her bowels were normal and her headaches were a lot better. Her bowels had improved substantially, but they were still a long way from functioning optimally. It took a few more months of fine-tuning her regimen and giving her body more time to restore balance to get her bowels truly functioning normally and for the headaches to resolve entirely. During that time, she told me how excited she was to be planning a trip to visit family who lived out of state, since she hadn't seen them in a long time. Her daughter also stated that her mother had returned to her more usual self and activities.

This may seem like an extreme case, but I see cases like this every day. The only thing extreme about this case is how long she suffered without seeking the help of a doctor. Most people seek help from multiple sources for these kinds of issues, which typically results in being on one or often multiple medications for the headaches, some of which cause constipation, so the constipation is blamed on that. Other medications are then prescribed, as well as blood pressure medications, sleep medications, and anxiety medications. Once a person starts down this path, it is not unusual to end up on six, eight, 10, or even more medications after many years. Whenever there is a long medication list, for a variety of conditions, make sure you consider if magnesium deficiency is playing a role in some of them.

# Is Magnesium Deficiency Causing Your Pain and Tension?

Without magnesium, your nervous system and muscles cannot relax. You likely know what "not relaxing" feels like: anxiety, irritability, poor sleep, and muscle tension/pain. Magnesium deficiency plays a huge role in how stress causes both muscle tension and mood tension.

**How do you know if you are deficient in magnesium?**
Magnesium deficiency could be playing a role in your health if you suffer from the following symptoms: anxiety, irritability, intense anger, short temper, restless sleep, panic attacks, muscle aches, restless leg syndrome, high blood pressure, heart palpitations, headaches or migraines, muscle tension, constipation, fibromyalgia, or menstrual cramps.

If you have many of these symptoms, magnesium deficiency could be making your symptoms worse. Some, or potentially all, of your symptoms will improve or fully resolve when you give your body the magnesium it needs.

Do NOT rely on blood tests: only magnesium levels that are dangerously low will show up on blood tests. Most people experience the painful symptoms of magnesium deficiency before it is severe enough to show up on blood tests.

**Causes of magnesium deficiency**
- Not eating enough leafy greens, beans and legumes, and nuts.
- Eating food grown in magnesium depleted soil. (Most U.S. soil is magnesium deficient.)
- Activity and stress increase the demand for magnesium.
- Excess calcium supplementation can induce relative magnesium deficiency.

**How to fix magnesium deficiency**

1. The first step to increase magnesium is food. Eating a whole foods diet rich in leafy greens, beans, legumes, and nuts supports optimal brain function.

2. You may benefit from supplementing magnesium. Magnesium supplementation is very safe for the same reason it can also be tricky: Magnesium stimulates bowel function. Work with a trained functional medicine doctor or naturopath to find the best dose for you.

3. If you are taking large doses of calcium, you will likely require higher doses of magnesium. Calcium and magnesium need to be used in the right amounts, in balance with each other. Seek the help of a trained functional medicine doctor or naturopath to determine the ideal doses of calcium and magnesium for you.

# Putting it all Together:

## Functional Medicine Diagnoses

How do all these basics, food, nutrients, sleep, and activities, come together to build health? The human body is a complex network of biochemical interactions which, when working well, create both mental and physical health. When there are disruptions, patterns of dysfunction and disease develop, resulting in both mental and physical symptoms. Recognizing some of these more common patterns of the vicious cycle of disease will help guide clinicians toward the necessary interventions for each person.

Sometimes people desire a deeper understanding of how imbalances in those basic nutrients actually disrupt the functioning of the body, and why addressing these issues is so important. Also, when people have been ill a long time, diseases can evolve to a level where more intervention than just the basics will be necessary.

First we will get an overview of the most common functional medicine diagnoses that cause so much of the suffering people with mental health conditions experience. The three major patterns of dysfunction that lead to symptoms of mental illness are:

- Blood sugar dysregulation
- Hormone imbalances
- Excess inflammation

For most people with specialized mental health training, making these diagnoses and treating them completely will require a referral to a doctor of functional medicine. But having a working knowledge of what patterns to look for will help clinicians educate and motivate people to make the nutritional and environmental changes that are necessary for the brain to function at its best.

# Blood Sugar Dysregulation and Reactive Hypoglycemia

Blood sugar is the fuel for the brain; without a steady supply of fuel, the brain functions poorly. Just like an engine, if there is too little or too much fuel, the engine sputters or even stops working until the problem is repaired. For the brain to function optimally, the supply of blood sugar needs to be just right—consistently. Blood sugar that is too high or too low, or rapidly swinging one direction or the other, impairs both mood and cognitive function. Those impairments look identical to the symptoms of some forms of ADHD, bipolar, excessive anger or irritability, and anxiety.

Regulation of blood sugar involves multiple organ systems: the pancreas, the adrenal glands, the brain, and the thyroid. When these systems are working well, the body keeps blood sugar in a very narrow range. Even when a person eats a lot of sugar all at once, blood sugar should not rise more than a couple of points. The same is true with the opposite kind of stress: if the body is forced to go without food, even for days, it will tap into its stores of energy and prevent blood sugar from dropping. However, both of these scenarios are big strains on blood sugar regulation, and such strains should be avoided!

When most people hear the term blood sugar, they associate it with diabetes. Diabetes is one type of impaired blood sugar regulation, and most diabetics have experienced blood sugar swings associated with impaired ability to regulate blood sugar.

> **But many people who do not have diabetes suffer symptoms that are the direct result of poor blood sugar regulation. In both groups, these symptoms are commonly attributed to something else: stress, hormones, other people's actions, ADHD, bipolar, or anxiety.**

If a person reports that their blood sugar has already been tested, and they were told it was normal, what that person had was a screening test for diabetes. But because many people who do not have diabetes can have reactive hypoglycemia, a more thorough test is used to identify reactive hypoglycemia. This test is called a glucose tolerance test and starts with testing fasting glucose like a diabetes screening test, but after that part of the test, the person stays at the lab and drinks a soda. The person continues to stay at the lab and their blood sugar is monitored for the next few hours. What should happen, even after drinking a lot of sugar, is the blood sugar should stay exactly the same. When the body is functioning as it was designed to function, it can maintain healthy blood sugar even after a big input of sugar. It requires activating multiple back-up systems, which is a big strain and not recommended to do often, but the body should be able to handle it. If the blood sugar fluctuates and drops significantly, the test is positive for reactive hypoglycemia.

How much stress the blood sugar regulation system can handle varies greatly. **In people who have poor blood sugar regulation, even small stresses, such as skipping one meal, or eating a sugary snack, will trigger reactive hypoglycemia and the associated symptoms.** The most common symptoms are feeling irritable, moody, and/or having trouble focusing or other symptoms of cognitive decline when a meal or snack is missed, or a couple hours after consuming sugar or a carbohydrate-only meal or snack. **Some people even feel shaky, anxious, or lose their temper in that situation.** Another common symptom is feeling tired or sleepy after eating, especially if the food eaten was sugary or starchy. In kids, the "sugar high" that often comes first may be as problematic for behavior as the crash that follows. Parents know that kids are often oblivious to these changes in behavior and mood that result from eating. The kicker is *many* adults suffer the same symptoms and are equally unaware just how much food and eating patterns affect how they feel.

**Often poor blood sugar regulation is the underlying root cause behind symptoms of ADHD, irritability, anxiety, and bipolar.** In those cases, steadying blood sugar will completely resolve the symptoms and make pharmaceutical treatment unnecessary. But even if blood sugar issues were not the initial cause of the problematic symptoms, people who suffer from ADHD or bipolar are much more prone to habits that trigger blood sugar swings, such as eating erratically or over-indulging in simple carbohydrates. Those blood sugar swings then worsen the person's symptoms. If the patient and doctor then mistakenly think that the medication is no longer working and raise the dose or change the medication, the real problem will not be addressed. Stabilizing blood sugar will help medications work more effectively, often at lower doses. When medications are effective at lower doses, their negative side-effects are often eliminated. The type of anxiety that is most likely to be caused by a blood sugar drop is anxiety "attacks." When people suddenly start feeling anxiety, or even panic, for no reason, the most likely cause for that feeling is a blood sugar drop. Stabilizing blood sugar will help the person recover from the episode faster, and preventing blood sugar swings will prevent the anxiety from starting.

## How to Regulate Blood Sugar

All the diet recommendations in Chapter 7 will help regulate blood sugar. But **people with blood sugar regulation issues need to focus extra attention on two specific aspects of eating:**

**1.** Eat balanced meals and snacks      **2.**      Eat frequently: every 2 to 4 hours

### Step 1: Eat Protein and Fiber as Part of Every Meal and Snack

Protein- and fiber-containing foods stabilize blood sugar. Food containing sugar or starch push blood sugar higher and then lower, increasing the severity of blood sugar swings and making you feel irritable, anxious, and shaky. Therefore, the best food choices are those that combine protein, fiber, and fat along with complex carbohydrates.

## Step 2: Eat Every 2 to 4 Hours

People don't have to eat a lot, but they do need to eat frequently. Eat within one hour of waking and continue to eat every two to four hours after. (Typically, every three to four hours is sufficient for adults; children need to eat every two to three hours.) Pack nutritious snacks to last throughout the day when on the go. Help people plan meal and snack times into their schedules. For people who forget to eat, have them use phone alarms as reminders to help them train themselves to eat regularly and experience how much better they feel when they do. Everyone needs to choose a few healthy options they like and make those their go-to munchies.

# Hormone Imbalances: A Hidden Cause of Mental Health Symptoms

Hormonal imbalances can cause many of the symptoms of depression, anxiety, bipolar, ADHD, and irritability. When the symptoms get severe enough, people often get prescribed medication to alter neurotransmitters. But as long as the hormones continue to disrupt neurotransmitters, the medications will at best diminish the symptoms, and usually lose effectiveness over time.

Even when hormonal imbalances are not the initial cause of symptoms of depression, anxiety, bipolar, irritability, or ADHD, living with these issues creates stress. Over time, that stress creates hormonal imbalances that mimic the original symptoms. Because the symptoms feel and look so similar, they are often misinterpreted as the disease worsening or medication losing effectiveness. However, when medication is increased or changed, without addressing the new underlying factors involved, it usually yields disappointing results. Only when all the underlying causes of the symptoms and the neurotransmitter imbalances are addressed, including the hormone factors, can the brain function at its best.

The most commonly recognized way that hormones create mental health symptoms is premenstrual syndrome (PMS) or premenstrual dysphoric disorder (PMDD). This is one common example, but there are many other ways that various hormones disrupt mood and interfere with mental clarity. Achieving hormone balance requires looking deeper than just the sex hormones. Thyroid and adrenal hormones also play critical roles in maintaining optimal mental and emotional functioning. In both men and women, thyroid, adrenal, and sex hormones are an interconnected system that regulates not just libido (and the menstrual cycle in women), but also metabolism, energy level, mental clarity, emotional stability, and the ability to handle stress.

Because the function of these hormones is to communicate with each other and respond to changes in the body, if there are problems in one area, inevitably problems will arise in other areas. Many symptoms blamed on menopause are the result of weak thyroid function. Without strong adrenal function, symptoms of low testosterone will develop. Understanding the role hormones are playing in your symptoms is not as easy as labeling a problem a "female hormone problem" or "thyroid problem."

> **These hormone imbalances are always interconnected and require a holistic approach, which examines all these complex relationships.**

Examining those interconnections requires understanding the hormone systems involved. Thyroid, adrenal, and sex hormones all play numerous complex roles in both physical and mental health. This section outlines their basic functions and the issues that most commonly present as mental health symptoms.

# Thyroid

Thyroid hormones regulate metabolism. The thyroid gland, in the throat, produces T4, which is then converted to the more active form, called T3, in the cells of the body. How much thyroid hormone the thyroid gland produces is regulated by the brain, specifically the pituitary gland and the hypothalamus sections. Symptoms of both high (hyperthyroidism) and low thyroid (hypothyroidism) can produce mental health symptoms. Several different problems with thyroid function can arise:

1. The thyroid gland stops producing enough thyroid hormone. Known as hypothyroidism, the cause can be autoimmune, iodine deficiency, or idiopathic (which means the cause cannot be identified).

   **Symptoms of hypothyroidism:**
   - Fatigue
   - Weight gain or difficulty losing weight
   - Constantly feeling cold or difficulty regulating body temperature
   - Loss of libido
   - Depression, apathy, or loss of motivation, feeling overwhelmed easily
   - Hair loss
   - Constipation
   - Dry skin
   - Brittle fingernails

   When people have all or most of the symptoms on this list (not just fatigue and difficulty losing weight), thyroid function needs to be thoroughly evaluated with blood tests. Even if TSH is normal, free T4 and free T3 also need to be tested to evaluate the ratios between the numbers to determine if thyroid support may still be beneficial even if medication is not needed.

2. The brain stops regulating the thyroid properly—called secondary hypothyroidism. The symptoms are similar to primary hypothyroidism.

3. The thyroid can overproduce thyroid hormone. Known as Grave's disease, or hyperthyroidism, this is an autoimmune disease.

**Symptoms of hyperthyroidism:**

- Anxiety
- Heart palpitations/racing heart
- Irritability
- Insomnia

- Weight loss
- Fatigue
- Sweating
- Sensitivity to heat

Hyperthyroidism is typically diagnosed quite easily with lab work. Hypothyroidism is much more commonly overlooked because many doctors screen for thyroid issues with just a TSH test. When people have all the symptoms of hypothyroidism (not just fatigue and difficulty losing weight!) but have been told their thyroid is normal, refer to a doctor of functional medicine who will analyze TSH, T4, and T3—and the ratios between them.

Undiagnosed (and therefore untreated) hypothyroidism is a significant cause of what gets labeled treatment-resistant depression. When the depression is due to low thyroid, no other therapy is going to help significantly or consistently. Undertreated hypothyroidism can create similar problems. If a person continues to suffer many of the symptoms of hypothyroidism despite treatment, also refer to a doctor of functional medicine.

Hashimoto's thyroiditis, an autoimmune disease, is one particular cause of hypothyroidism. Because it is an autoimmune disease, it needs not only the treatments already discussed, but also all the interventions in Chapter 16 for reducing excess inflammation.

# Adrenal

The adrenal glands manage how the body responds to stress. "Stress" includes big emotional stressors, such as losing a job or a death in the family, but it also includes physical stresses, such as standing up from sitting down or shifting from a warm indoor environment to a cold outdoor environment. All of these stresses, large and small, emotional and physical, require adaptation by the body to maintain equilibrium. When the adrenal glands are functioning well, small stressors go unnoticed, and people feel capable of dealing with the larger ones. When adrenal glands are functioning poorly, even small stresses can feel overwhelming.

The adrenal gland produces several different hormones, as well as other messengers, which regulate many different pathways in the body. There are three primary hormones, which, if not regulated efficiently, can cause symptoms of anxiety and panic attacks, sleep disruption, depression, ADHD, and bipolar.

1. **Epinephrine** (adrenaline) is the fast-acting stress response hormone. When one is faced with danger, epinephrine immediately focuses attention and energizes the body into the well-known "fight or flight" response. When there is real and imminent danger, this response can be life-saving. But if this response is triggered by non-dangerous situations, people may experience a panic attack or a PTSD flashback.

2. **Cortisol** responds to longer-term stress. It doesn't produce nearly as instantaneous nor as dramatic a response as epinephrine, but it lasts longer. Cortisol also plays a key role

in regulating circadian rhythm (sleep/wake cycle). Part of the circadian rhythm is an increase in melatonin and decrease in cortisol in the evening to induce relaxation and sleepiness. If cortisol stays elevated due to stress, the sleep cycle will likely be affected. This is the biological mechanism that causes people to have trouble sleeping when feeling stressed. Again this is a life-saving adaptation; staying alert in the face of danger is critical. However, if cortisol is staying elevated unnecessarily, because the adrenals are not well-regulated, the sleep loss can start to feed a downward spiral of dysfunction. Even when the cortisol response is appropriate, the body cannot maintain this adaptation forever, and eventually health starts to suffer.

3. **DHEA** is the precursor to the sex hormones. If insufficient or irregular DHEA is being made, it will disrupt the balance of sex hormones in both men and women. DHEA is the link between adrenal function and regulating sex hormones.

## Adrenal Dysregulation: Wired AND Tired

Several different problems can affect the adrenal glands. They can be over-active, which is called Cushing's disease, and is rare. They can also fail entirely, which is called Addison's disease. Addison's disease is fatal without treatment, but fortunately the conventional medical world is quite good at recognizing and treating Addison's disease. What is far more common is adrenal dysregulation: when the adrenals are still working, but not with 100 percent efficiency and efficacy. Also called adrenal dysfunction or adrenal fatigue, this problem affects a huge number of people and has tremendous impact on mental health.

**Adrenal dysregulation symptoms:**
- Fatigue: generally throughout the day, or periods of good energy alternating with periods of poor energy; also can be needing coffee to get going in the morning
- Poor focus, sometimes experienced as "brain fog"
- Depression, lack of motivation, feeling overwhelmed, apathetic or hopeless about stressors
- Difficulty making decisions
- Insomnia: difficulty falling asleep or difficulty staying asleep (waking in the middle of the night and having trouble falling back to sleep)
- Irritability or oversensitivity
- Impulsiveness
- Anxiety or panic attacks
- PMS symptoms

Adrenal dysregulation impacts nearly every aspect of mental and emotional health. So often the symptoms of anxiety, bipolar, irritability, depression, and ADHD are actually different manifestations of adrenal dysregulation. Even when it did not initially cause the symptoms, living with those issues is stressful and strains adrenal function, causing adrenal dysregulation to become part of perpetuating the problem. People in both scenarios will benefit from adrenal support to diminish symptoms and restore balance.

# How to Restore Adrenal Function

The good news is that adrenal function can be improved, even restored to youthful levels, with good self-care. The basics of adrenal support are the nutritional and lifestyle issues that have already been discussed. Without adequate sleep, healthy meals including B-vitamins, and exercise, the adrenals will not be able to function properly. Supporting healthy adrenal function and resiliency to stress is *why* these factors are critical to life.

Caffeine elimination is often part of treating the sleep issues that are part of the vicious cycle of adrenal dysfunction because caffeine is an adrenal stimulant. People reach for caffeine when they are tired or stressed because caffeine pushes the adrenals to work harder, much like whipping a horse to make it run faster. However, it only works temporarily; eventually it overwhelms the adrenals' ability to regulate and starts to become part of the problem. Restoring natural, complete, adrenal function will often require reducing or eliminating caffeine, at least temporarily.

Stress management techniques are also part of basic adrenal support. When people have more skills to cope with stress, it lessens the demand on the adrenals. As the adrenals start to function better, people will become more capable of utilizing stress management techniques. Treating the adrenals both physically and psychologically is the way to stop the downward spiral of stress causing health problems and start to turn it around.

Every human requires daily attention to these basics to optimize both mental and physical health. For many people, that effort will be enough to break out of the downward spiral and restore health. But some people will need more than the basics. People who have been under extreme or long-term stress will still need to address the basics, but may need more support to really restore optimal functioning.

Numerous adaptogen herbs support adrenal function. These are available over-the-counter, but still need to be used correctly. Depending on which phase of adrenal dysregulation a person is in, different adaptogen herbs will work more effectively. When used incorrectly, or during the wrong phase, potentially they can make a person feel worse. When a person is addressing all the basics of adrenal support and still experiencing the symptoms of adrenal dysregulation, refer to a doctor of functional medicine for more advanced adrenal support.

# Male and Female Sex Hormones (Testosterone, Estrogen, Progesterone)

The familiar symptoms of male and female sex hormone imbalance are right on the surface: irritability, moodiness, anxiety, fatigue, depression, and changes in libido. What can be more hidden is what is causing the disruption in those hormones—very often it is undiagnosed adrenal or thyroid issues. In these cases, interventions such as hormone therapy (birth control pills or hormone replacement therapy for women, testosterone therapy for men) can help for a while, but will not work long-term if the thyroid and adrenal issues are not addressed. This is true at all stages of life, in both men and women. Even most menopausal symptoms are the result of untreated adrenal dysregulation (and possibly hypothyroidism as well). Therefore it is critical to address all the hormone systems to fully respond to sex hormone issues, even when using hormone therapy is clinically indicated.

# Balancing Inflammation for Better Health

Understanding how inflammation contributes to disease, both mental and physical, is currently a topic of intense research. Current science only understands the tip of the iceberg about the numerous and diverse cellular and biochemical interactions that constitute inflammation and all the various ways environment, genetics, and epigenetics influence these pathways. Despite this intricate network of complexities, there are three critical facts to understand about inflammation:

1. Inflammation is a healing process; without inflammation, the body cannot heal from injuries or infections.

2. Inflammation can turn into "excess inflammation" or "chronic inflammation" when the inflammatory process simultaneously creates further damage during the healing process.

3. Foods and nutrients dramatically shift the body's balance of inflammation— inflammatory foods lead to chronic inflammation, pain, and faster aging, while nutrient-rich foods promote healing by restoring balance to the inflammation pathways.

## Causes of Excess Inflammation

Excess inflammation arises from many different sources. In most cases, several of these causes are contributing to a person's symptoms by the time someone is suffering enough to seek help. Each will need to be investigated and addressed to fully restore balance. Addressing only one or some of them but ignoring others will likely yield unsatisfactory results.

### Food Sensitivities

Chemicals in the food supply and even foods themselves can trigger excess inflammation. What triggers a reaction in one person may not be a problem for other people. Some people will react to chemicals like food colorings while others will not. Chemical sweeteners and preservatives can also trigger inflammatory reactions in some people. No one needs any of these chemicals, so it is always safe and advisable to avoid them.

Common foods that can cause inflammatory responses in some people are gluten, corn, dairy, soy, and the nightshade vegetables. Just because gluten (or any of the others) can cause a reaction in some people does not mean that is a problem for everyone. A food that is healthy for one person may be damaging for another. Just because some people have a reaction to gluten, that does not mean that "gluten-free" is synonymous with healthy; in fact, many gluten-free products are even more damaging than the originals they replaced.

### Dysbiosis

Dysbiosis is an umbrella term for any kind of imbalance in the bacteria that live in the digestive tract. Known as the gut microbiome, these bacteria are a critical part of digestion and overall health. The human digestive tract needs to have the right bacteria residing there and *not* have the wrong bacteria present. Any disruption to this balance is called dysbiosis. Dysbiosis compromises digestive function, which can impact the break-down and absorption of nutrients, leading to nutritional deficiencies. Dysbiosis can also result in the release of toxins, which can impact brain function.

### Toxins

Toxins come from a variety of sources, both outside and inside the body. Toxins resulting from dysbiosis can be absorbed into the blood stream and affect brain function in a variety of ways. Environmental toxins can also be ingested through food, absorbed through the skin, or breathed in through the lungs. Different toxins impact different inflammatory pathways and affect people differently, so much more needs to be studied about these interactions.

### Trauma

Trauma by definition is a cause of excess inflammation. A trauma is an injury that exceeds the body's ability to heal on its own. When the inflammatory pathways that are designed to heal get overwhelmed and cannot complete the job, excess inflammation can result. Physical trauma is a major cause of excess inflammation. But physical trauma is not the only cause—psychological trauma also causes excess inflammation.

Emotional injuries that did not involve any physical injury have been shown to trigger some of the same inflammatory pathways as physical trauma (Rosen et al., 2017). Because there is no physical trauma to heal, the inflammatory reactions actually cause physical damage rather than heal it. This link is why so many people with trauma histories experience chronic pain. If those people get told, "It's all in your head," that is false. The original injury was to the mind, but it translates into physical changes that cause very real excess inflammation and pain.

## Symptoms of Excess Inflammation

The main symptoms of chronic inflammation are pain and poor healing. Anyone who experiences chronic pain has some form of chronic excess inflammation. Old injuries that never fully healed are a source of excess inflammation. Poor healing of new injuries also indicates dysfunction in the inflammatory pathways. Poor healing is relative to the injury:

A paper cut should heal in a couple days; if it is still present after a couple of weeks, something is wrong. A badly sprained ankle will not heal in a few weeks; it is expected to take a few months. But if it is still painful and swollen after a year, something is wrong in the inflammatory pathways.

Autoimmune disease is the end-stage of excess inflammation. In autoimmune disease, not only have the inflammatory pathways failed to heal an injury, they are so out of balance that they start to create further injury. This further injury then triggers more inflammation, which triggers further injury, and another vicious cycle has been created. There are many different pathways that can be involved, which is why there are many different kinds of autoimmune disease, but what they all have in common is that the body is damaging itself.

Not everyone who has excess inflammation has it severely enough to have an autoimmune disease. More common and vague symptoms such as fatigue, obesity, digestive symptoms, allergies, irritability, depression, bipolar, anxiety, ADHD, and insomnia can all be related to excess inflammation. Doctors don't typically think of mental/emotional symptoms as being related to the physical aspects of inflammation, but it always needs to be looked for.

## Restoring Balance to Inflammation

Despite many anti-inflammatory drugs, the reason excess inflammation continues to be a growing problem is that no drug can ever restore balance to a complex system. **Drugs block individual inflammatory pathways, which can relieve symptoms related to overactivity of that pathway, but they never treat why the pathway was overactive in the first place.** When the root cause is not addressed, the disease progresses and the drug tends to lose effectiveness over time. Also, when one individual pathway is blocked, it can further disrupt the delicate balance of how all the different pathways influence each other. This disruption is why so many anti-inflammatory medications have been linked to unwanted, and sometimes even dangerous, side effects.

**The key to restoring balance to the inflammatory pathways is food.** This is yet another reason why a healthy, whole foods diet is critical. Anti-inflammatory diets always start with the healthy, whole foods diet outlined in Chapter 7 and are then customized to meet any specific needs of an individual. Getting people started with the core approach is a critical first step that all other steps build on. For many people, diet alone will be enough to resolve the symptoms of excess inflammation. Other people will need more advanced work with a doctor of functional medicine to determine what individual customizations may be necessary.

# Treating Chronic Pain

Chapter

# 17

Too many people suffer from chronic pain, and the mental health effects of chronic physical pain are both varied and severe. This common etiology must *always* be addressed because even low levels of pain take a high toll on mood and energy. Some people do not address the pain and simply live with it, for a variety of reasons. There may be fear of the diagnosis or certain potential treatments, and other times people simply do not know how to address it or who to ask about it or that there may be other ways to address it if the first treatment failed. Sometimes people have lived with chronic pain so long they do not even identify it as pain, and may not complain about it.

**Chronic pain has a huge number of multi-factorial causes, but it always indicates some form of chronic inflammation.** Depending on the form of inflammation, different interventions may be indicated, but all of them are more likely to be effective when people are eating an anti-inflammatory diet. Even though not all pain can be fixed by diet alone, it is so often the piece that is overlooked that prevents other treatments from working fully.

**Action Items:**

1. *Start with helping people eat an anti-inflammatory diet.*
2. *Help people access appropriate medical care for their condition.*
3. *Provide psychological tools to help them cope with the presence of chronic pain.*

## When There is Atypical Onset of Symptoms: Could it be Lyme Disease?

Lyme disease is multiplying rapidly in many parts of the country, and "neuro-Lyme," which often presents primarily as mental/emotional symptoms first, is also becoming more common. Because people with neuro-Lyme often do not have the symptoms of rash, fever, and joint pain that are most commonly associated with Lyme, they end up in the office of a mental health professional instead of a doctor.

Lyme disease is *not* the issue in most cases of anxiety, or bipolar, ADHD, depression, or irritability. But when people present with sudden, atypical syndromes of mental illness, most commonly including anxiety and moodiness, Lyme disease should be considered. People will often say things like, "What is my problem? I used to be able to handle all of this, and now I can't handle anything, and nothing has really changed," meaning there are no new stresses that may account for the change in emotional state. They can also identify exactly when the change happened, which may or may not be associated with a minor illness (which they only paid attention to in hindsight).

## Action Item:

*In atypical presentation of anxiety with rapid onset despite no identifiable trigger, question if Lyme disease could be the reason. Refer to a Lyme-literate doctor.*

# Find and Treat the Cause:

## The Questions to Answer, Organized by Diagnosis

When practicing any form of medicine, it is critically important to always be treating a person, not a diagnosis. The diagnosis is only the first step to understanding what is going on with the person and how to help them. Determining the diagnosis presents a variety of challenges. People can present with different symptoms on different days, making it hard to really find the core of the case. With all the focus on diagnosis in clinical practice, all too often both patients and practitioners get seduced into believing that an accurate diagnosis is the same thing as understanding what is going wrong and how to fix it. Rarely does this happen in the world of mental illness. Most mental health diagnoses categorize and label the symptoms, but do not explain them.

To know how to help a given individual, regardless of diagnosis, clinicians need to repeatedly ask, "What is *causing* these symptoms?" That question needs to be asked repeatedly because there is almost always more than one correct answer to that question, and sometimes the question has different answers at various times. Especially when people have been ill for a long time, quite often the factors that initially caused the problem are different from the factors that are perpetuating the problem.

> The goal is to find all the different answers to that question, "Why?" and then develop an understanding of how each issue affects the others. Understanding the positive feedback loops (vicious cycles) will reveal the treatments necessary to help people break out of the downward spiral and start healing.

The diagnosis does provide some direction as to which common causes of symptoms need to be investigated to determine which issues are affecting each unique patient. The rest of this section will review the major categories of diagnoses and outline the questions that should be asked to determine the causes underlying the person's suffering.

Following each major category of diagnoses, an overview of the primary questions to answer will be listed in order of priority. The questions at the top are the ones that are most likely playing a role and will lead to effective treatment. However, to fully help someone reach optimal health and fully achieve their potential, all of the questions must be considered. Because most of these underlying imbalances can cause a variety of symptoms and manifest differently in people, many of the questions will be found under more than one diagnosis. Particularly in people who suffer more than one diagnosis, analyzing where the common etiologies are will provide clues as to which issues are most likely the underlying causes in that case.

# Treating Depression

> - Is there B-vitamin insufficiency?
> - Is the person eating adequate protein?
> - Are Acid-blocking medications being taken long-term?
> - Is the thyroid functioning optimally?
> - Is it postpartum depression, or did the symptoms start in the first year postpartum?
> - Is vitamin D level optimized?
> - Is the person engaging in physical movement?
> - Is there essential fatty acid deficiency?
> - Does the person get adequate amounts of refreshing sleep?

## Is There B-Vitamin Insufficiency?

There are several different B-vitamins and multiple ways that insufficiencies can cause depression. In cases of situational depression, the increased B-vitamin demands of stress may be overwhelming dietary intake, particularly if the person eats a lot of processed foods. During times of stress, making an effort to consume extra B-vitamins will increase the chances that the body has the raw materials it needs to manage the stress effectively.

Some people need higher amounts of B-vitamins to function at their best, even under optimal conditions. For these people, a standard American diet will not provide enough B-vitamins. The combination of increased B-vitamin requirement and depleted diet puts them at increased risk of long-term clinical depression, and those people need to make an extra effort to ensure adequate B-vitamin consumption, consistently. When stress is high in people who already require higher amounts of B-vitamins every day, the need is that much more difficult to meet, and they have an even greater risk of suffering from depression.

In addition to assessing diet for general B-vitamin consumption, B12 should also be tested when there is progressive, non-transient depression. (Sometimes antidepressant medications can help temporarily, but the efficacy always wanes over time because the medication is not treating the real cause when the depression is due to B12 deficiency.) Typically, B12-deficiency depression is accompanied by significant physical fatigue and will progress to neuropathy (nerve damage) if left untreated. The most common cause of

B12-deficient depression is pernicious anemia, which typically onsets later in life. However, B12 deficiency is occurring more frequently in younger people because of the rise in rates of inflammatory diseases, both autoimmune disease and inflammatory bowel disease. (Bariatric surgery is another rapidly increasing cause of B12 deficiency in people of all ages.)

The only dietary cause of B12 deficiency is strict veganism. People who follow a strict vegan diet need to supplement B12 with either nutritional supplements or specially formulated nutritional yeast.

Folic acid is another individual B-vitamin that may need to be evaluated in complicated or treatment-resistant cases. People who have mutations in the MTHFR gene have a compromised ability to turn folic acid into its active form, called 5-MTHF. Lack of 5-MTHF can disrupt the production of multiple neurotransmitters, including serotonin, dopamine, and norepinephrine. When people have treatment-resistant depression or depression that is complicated by multiple co-morbidities, refer to a psychiatrist who does MTHFR testing and appropriate treatment. See Chapter 11 for more complete details on evaluating B12 and folic acid.

### Action Items:

1. *In situational depression, assess diet for daily intake of B-vitamins. Consider a B-complex supplement if intake is marginal or stress is very high.*

2. *In clinical depression, assess diet for daily intake of B-vitamins. Help people eat whole grains, beans, legumes, and nuts on a daily basis. Consider a trial with a therapeutic dose of a B-complex supplement, especially if intake is marginal or stress is very high.*

3. *In longer-term, non-transient depression, make sure the PCP or psychiatrist involved has checked B12 level and is treating it appropriately if the level is less than 450pg/mL. Also consider B-complex supplement along with B12 treatment.*

4. *When depression is resistant to treatment and/or complicated by multiple co-morbidities, refer to a psychiatrist who does MTHFR testing.*

## Does the Person Eat Adequate Protein?

Protein provides the amino acid building blocks to make neurotransmitters. Insufficient dietary protein will cause neurotransmitter deficiencies. (In the case of depression, serotonin is the most relevant neurotransmitter.) Animal products, including fish, chicken, turkey, pork, and eggs are the densest sources of protein. Soy is also a rich source of protein, particularly tofu, tempeh, and edamame. It is possible to get adequate protein from a purely plant-based diet, but vegetarians need to pay closer attention to how much protein they are eating, and with extra focus on the beans, legumes, soy, and protein-rich whole grains that are part of a healthy, whole foods diet.

### Action Item:

*Make sure the person is eating a minimum of 50 grams of protein per day, ideally evenly spaced across all meals.*

# Are Acid-Blocking Medications Being Taken Long-Term?

Protein pump inhibitors (PPIs) and H2 blockers are two different classes of medications that are used to treat heartburn, reflux, and GERD. They are available in both prescription and over-the-counter strengths. **Short-term use of these medications is safe, but long-term use can interfere with nutrient absorption leading to deficiencies in vitamins, minerals, and amino acids, all of which can contribute to depression.**

Many people (but not all) who are self-treating with these medications will be able to wean off them simply by switching to a whole foods diet. Others will need additional support from functional medicine to fully heal. If a doctor (PCP or gastroenterologist) has prescribed any of these medications long-term, it is critical to work with a functional medicine doctor to fully heal the digestive tract, ensuring safety and optimizing long-term health.

### Action Item:

*Ask patients if they are taking any of these medications and, if so, how long. If the person is struggling with discontinuing their over-the-counter self-medication or if their doctor has prescribed long-term use, refer to a functional medicine doctor.*

# Is the Thyroid Functioning Optimally?

Some of the primary symptoms of low thyroid (hypothyroid) are low mood, apathy, lack of motivation, and depression. Because some of the other symptoms of hypothyroidism overlap with symptoms of depression (fatigue, pain, and loss of libido), all too often these symptoms get blamed on the depression rather than hypothyroidism. Even people who have been screened for thyroid disorders are often tested inadequately, and the thyroid problem gets missed and goes untreated. When other interventions are tried, they either do not help or only help temporarily, leading to a diagnosis of treatment-resistant depression. The core treatment necessary in these cases is appropriate thyroid support.

### Action Item:

*Check for other symptoms of hypothyroid and, if they are present, help the patient get a thorough thyroid evaluation by a functional medicine doctor.*

# Is it Postpartum Depression, or Did the Depression Start in the First Year Postpartum?

Postpartum depression, even if it has lasted past the postpartum window, is a sign of adrenal dysfunction. The physical, emotional, and hormonal stress of pregnancy, delivery, and caring for an infant qualifies as a major stressor and, in some women, will require adrenal support. When postpartum depression extends past the first year postpartum, the underlying cause is still the same and needs to be treated with adrenal support. Work with the self-care fundamentals that are extra challenging during this period: adequate sleep, eating regular and balanced meals, daily activity, and stress management. Support during this phase can make an enormous difference not just for the woman with postpartum depression, but for her whole family.

**Action Item:**

> *When stress is contributing to depression symptoms, provide basic adrenal support: work with any issues needed around adequate sleep, balanced and regular meals, daily exercise, and stress management. Refer to a functional medicine doctor or naturopath if more intensive support is needed.*

## Is Vitamin D Level Optimized?

Suboptimal vitamin D levels are extremely common and are correlated with higher rates of depression and seasonal affective disorder (SAD). More importantly, despite all the controversy around vitamin D, restoring vitamin D to optimal levels has been shown to improve depression. Vitamin D is made when certain skin cells are exposed to ultraviolet light (sunlight). Therefore, the ways to increase vitamin D are through increased sun exposure or supplements. However, the risk associated with excess sun exposure (skin cancer, skin aging) are well known, and taking excess supplements can lead to vitamin D toxicity. The safest way to optimize vitamin D is to work with a doctor who will test and determine optimal vitamin D dosing for each individual to maintain long-term health.

**Action Item:**

> *Have patients work with their primary care physician to have vitamin D tested and maintained in the optimal range of 45 to 65ng/mL.*

## Is the Person Engaging in Physical Movement?

The research evaluating the effectiveness of exercise in improving depression is significant and overwhelmingly positive. **Specifically, high intensity activity (getting out of breath) changes neurotransmitters and hormones in multiple ways that diminish the symptoms of depression.**

For an overview of how to address physical movement in depression, revisit how to use the various tools and strategies discussed in Chapter 6.

## Is There Essential Fatty Acid Deficiency?

The most common fat deficiency in mental health disorders, particularly bipolar, depression, and ADHD, is lack of eicosapentaenoic acid (EPA) and docosahexaenoic acid (DHA).

For a full overview of how essential fatty acids affect depression and other aspects of mental health, review the details of Chapter 8.

# Does the Person Get
# Adequate Amounts of Refreshing Sleep?

One of the many effects of inadequate or poor sleep is mood disturbance and low mood. Many people do not realize they are not getting adequate sleep and do not identify it as a problem. Sometimes people even complain that depression is causing them to sleep too much, when more sleep is exactly what they need to help the depression. Always ask about sleep amount and sleep quality, even when people do not complain about it. Help people experiment with getting more sleep if they are getting less than nine hours per night, or even more if they have been sleep-deprived.

When people are struggling with difficulty sleeping, go back to the basics. Evaluate sleep environment and bedtime routine and help people make any necessary changes. If the person is consuming any form of caffeine (coffee, tea, energy drinks, soda, or pills), educate them about the secondary effects of caffeine and debunk any myths they may believe (see Chapter 5). Don't underestimate how powerful working with the basics can be: many people struggle deeply with them and you will likely be the first person to address them meaningfully.

**Action Item:**

*Work with the four fundamental components of sleep. Help people make sleep a priority and overcome the obstacles that interfere with quality sleep.*

## CASE STUDY
# Depression and Adrenal Fatigue

Jim was referred to me by his marriage counselor. At age 56, he and his wife had started counseling, and it was the therapist's opinion that part of the bigger issue was that Jim suffered from depression, and treating his depression was necessary for the couple to make any progress. Jim had first sought help from his PCP, who had prescribed Lexapro. Jim had taken the Lexapro for a couple of months, but said he "didn't like how it made [him] feel," so he had stopped taking it. When he said he really didn't want to try any other meds, his therapist suggested trying a more holistic approach.

Jim claimed that he wasn't depressed, it was "just the situation." The situation was that he had three children, all of them teenagers. The oldest was 19 and suffered an autism spectrum disorder, still lived at home, and was unable to live independently. Jim and his wife were both struggling with how to help their son transition into adulthood, and their ideas about how to best deal with the situation were significantly different. This stress, and the conflict around it, had led them to marriage counseling.

Despite all the stress, Jim understood the value of self-care. He went to the gym most days, tried to eat healthily, and maintained a healthy weight. He typically went to bed by 10 pm, with his alarm set for 6:30 am, but he often woke up at 3 or 4 am and sometimes had trouble falling back asleep. He claimed his energy was pretty good, though if he didn't sleep well, he knew he was more irritable and less patient with both his family and co-workers.

Jim looked and acted like the picture of health, but as I talked to him more about his situation, his weariness started to show through. He admitted that he felt like he had tried everything, and that he didn't feel like it mattered what he did, so he had stopped trying. He was going to therapy because his wife wanted him to, but he didn't think it would or could actually help.

Clearly, Jim fit the criteria for situational depression, but the underlying cause in this case was adrenal fatigue. The chronic stress of the last two decades, combined with the current acute stress, had accumulated to the point where his reserves were waning and he could no longer respond the way he used to. The best way to treat this kind of depression is with adrenal support.

Jim had already done a fair amount of adrenal support on his own; he had learned long ago that when he started feeling anxious, the most effective thing he could do was go work out. This strategy had gotten him through some earlier rough times, and anxiety was no longer an issue for him. But one of his more recent attempts to improve his health and mood was actually contributing to the situation. In an effort to eat healthier, he had mostly stopped eating grains and beans, and these are two primary sources of B-vitamins. This change was done with the best of intentions, but it was part of why he had progressed to a later stage of adrenal fatigue, despite doing so many other things correctly, such as eating plenty of protein and essential fatty acids.

I started Jim on B-complex to correct that issue. And because the stress had been going on so long and progressed to this level despite his basically healthy lifestyle, I also gave him ginseng, an adaptogen that boosts mood and energy by supporting adrenal function. Because he was often waking up too early, I also recommended he stop all caffeine to see if his sleep improved.

One month later, Jim reported that he noticed he had a little more patience for his kids and he didn't get so easily aggravated. Certainly this was a sign of improvement, but also not enough to solve the situation. As I talked to him more, a subtle but critical change in his outlook surfaced: he had noticed that when he was more patient with his kids, they responded differently, and so did his wife. Most importantly, he cared again. He was once again engaged with his family, and while that alone did not provide any answers, it did provide a place to start working.

A few months later, Jim asked a question that a lot of people ask: "How long do I have to keep doing this?" The answer is simple, but also vague: "As long as it's necessary." How long depends on many factors: the person's other physical health issues, their stress level, their social support system, and the availability of effective psychotherapy.

Like many people, Jim thought of himself as healthy and didn't want to "have to take anything." I advised him not to stop taking the supplements because he was still carrying a very high stress load, and I wanted him to continue to have the support he needed to work all the way through it.

Despite that, as things got better, he drifted away from the supplements. But a couple months later, he returned, because along with the help of his therapist he realized he was falling back into old habits, and they were indeed contributing to the conflict in his marriage and difficulties with his kids.

We restarted adrenal support, and again they helped. In this case, it took about a year for Jim and his wife to reconnect, learn how to communicate better, and then tackle their challenges. But when they did this, they did come up with a plan for their son that was acceptable to everyone, and in the end reduced the stress substantially. This was the desired result and also the point at which adrenal support can often be reduced to simple healthy lifestyle.

But during this process, another critical shift had happened: Jim no longer took his health for granted. Instead of asking, "Why do I have to do this?" he started asking, "What should I be doing to feel my best and perform my best, for myself, and my family?" At that point, he actually didn't want to stop the adrenal supplements! Despite that, I did wean him off the ginseng and talked more about how to get the nutrients he needed from food. But he also chose to take a high-quality multi-vitamin that contained much higher than average B vitamins, so that when stress levels increased, he would already be prepared and not be caught by surprise.

# Treating Anxiety

> - Are sleep and adrenal function being optimized?
> - Is there a magnesium deficiency?
> - Is there female hormone imbalance?
> - Is reactive hypoglycemia causing or exacerbating the symptoms?
> - Is there neurosensitivity to chemicals?

## Are Sleep and Adrenal Function Being Optimized?

Asking which came first, the adrenal issues or the anxiety, is like asking which came first, the chicken or the egg? The fact that sleep issues plague almost everyone who suffers from anxiety is another element common to the vicious cycle. The way to stop the downward spiral is by supporting adrenal function.

Eliminating caffeine is a critical first step when treating anxiety. Caffeine exacerbates anxiety and sleep disturbance, and strains adrenals. While people with anxiety often feel they can't live without their caffeine, the opposite is typically true: they live far more comfortably and effectively when they experiment with using less or none.

When people truly love their coffee or tea, switching to decaf is a way to enjoy the positive ritual that often develops around these beverages while eliminating the negative effects. Decaffeinated coffee and tea do contain tiny amounts of caffeine, but for the vast majority of people, it's not enough to cause problems.

**Action Items:**

1. *Initiate basic adrenal support:*
   - *adequate sleep*
   - *healthy meals*
   - *exercise*
   - *stress management techniques*
2. *Eliminate all forms of caffeine.*
3. *Consider more extensive adrenal support, with herbs like ashwagandha.*

## Is There a Magnesium Deficiency?

Because magnesium is necessary to relax, magnesium deficiency is a direct cause of anxiety. Even if it is not the only cause, because anxiety almost always has multiple contributing causes, magnesium deficiency will make the symptoms worse. Magnesium deficiency can also contribute to a wide variety of other health conditions that cause pain and anxiety, further exacerbating the anxiety.

To review how magnesium deficiency contributes to anxiety, return to Chapter 13 for full assessment and treatment details.

## Is There Female Hormone Imbalance?

Female hormone imbalances are well known to cause anxiety and many other mood disturbances in women and girls. If the anxiety is associated with the premenstrual phase, or is worse around that time, female hormones are likely part of the problem but not the only hormones involved. If it is a new symptom around menopause, female hormones, or other hormones (adrenal and thyroid), are playing a role. If anxiety is a new symptom around menopause, not only female hormones but other hormones, including adrenal and/or thyroid hormone imbalances all need to be evaluated and treated as necessary.

Treating with birth control pills or hormone replacement therapy can be very helpful. However, if they are the only interventions used, the results are likely to be temporary or incomplete. Fully addressing female hormone imbalances requires an examination of the deeper relationship between female hormones, adrenal hormones, and thyroid hormones.

### Action Item:

*If female hormone imbalance appears to be part of the problem, or even if it has already been identified as part of the problem, refer to functional or naturopathic medicine.*

## Is Reactive Hypoglycemia Causing or Exacerbating Symptoms?

When anxiety comes on suddenly for no apparent reason, which people may describe as an anxiety "attack" (or even a panic attack), hypoglycemia is one of the more likely causes. Especially if the person can't identify what they are anxious about, or why they are anxious, a drop in blood sugar is the most likely explanation for the feeling.

To review how to identify and treat reactive hypoglycemia, return to Chapter 14 for the full explanation.

## CASE STUDY
# Alice's Anxiety

Alice sought my help at age 48 because she didn't want to go back on anxiety medication. She had taken Xanax in the past, and it helped, but she was very afraid of the long-term side effects associated with the benzodiazepines. As stress intensified and other medical issues worsened, sleep issues were getting worse. She fully realized she was in a downward spiral, and that the lack of sleep was making her more anxious, as well as sicker, and that being more anxious and in more pain made the sleep worse, but she didn't know what else to do.

I asked Alice to start at the beginning so I could fully understand the progression of her myriad of symptoms. She said she grew up in an abusive household, and that even as a kid she was very anxious. She first started taking psychiatric medications when she was in her 20s, and at first she thought they helped, but as time went on she felt they weren't really solving the problem, just making it slightly more manageable. She also developed irritable bowel syndrome (IBS), then fibromyalgia, then interstitial cystitis. She said she went to at least 15 different doctors during her 30s, but no one could explain why she had these diseases or what was causing them. Medications didn't work, and she just continued to feel worse and worse.

She was stressed about her health and stressed about her marriage. Both her mental and physical symptoms were a point of conflict in her marriage, and that conflict made her feel even more anxious. More recently, her mother's health was also deteriorating, and spending more time caring for her mother was re-opening many childhood wounds as well as creating more conflict within her marriage.

With all of this, she felt like she was constantly anxious and was having full panic attacks at least once a week. This was the symptom that was making her consider taking Xanax again. She had been taking hormone replacement therapy for the past four years, which had helped both the anxiety and sleep at first, but now she was in constant pain from the fibromyalgia and interstitial cystitis. She was constantly tired, but would wake up almost every hour and often have trouble falling back asleep, despite taking female hormones. On top of all of these issues, she had read about how not getting adequate sleep contributed to weight gain, and that was one more issue that she struggled with to no avail—she had tried lots of different diets but had not only failed to lose weight, she was gaining weight.

How do you know where to start on cases like this? It can seem overwhelming, and most certainly the patient does feel very stuck. But in reality, the development of her symptoms also lays out the path to recovery. Early stress, even in childhood, strained her adrenal system. Her need to always be on alert kept her adrenals working overtime.

Because she often felt tired, she would drink coffee, which helped her feel better, but also heightened her anxiety, though she had never made that connection. Going on crash diets had further contributed to blood sugar swings and adrenal fatigue, as well as nutrient deficiency. Likely, she had suffered from magnesium deficiency for most of her life. The magnesium deficiency contributed to the fibromyalgia, and of course, being in pain worsened her stress and anxiety.

Eating an extremely low fat diet contributed to inflammation within her body, and eating products with NutraSweet also dramatically increased inflammation, until she was in nearly constant pain from fibromyalgia and interstitial cystitis. The IBS symptoms were the first warning signs, but then they caused further inflammation because her digestive tract could no longer efficiently absorb the few nutrients she did eat.

Therefore, the place to start is an anti-inflammatory diet, along with stopping caffeine. I gave her a diet plan because she felt constantly stressed about what to eat. I also wanted to give her examples of eating real food, instead of relying on the chemical sweeteners that were directly contributing to both her anxiety and her pain. I also had her switch to decaf coffee because she really enjoyed coffee, but the caffeine was contributing to her anxiety and her sleep issues. I also started her on magnesium and fish oil because her diet had been so deficient in these for so long that I wanted to help her feel better as quickly as possible.

A few weeks later, she said her pain was a little better, and that it was the first time that had happened in many years. But she complained that she was even more tired without the caffeine, and that the diet plan was just too hard to follow. She was anxious that if she ate all this food, she would gain weight. It took some pointed questions about her responses to certain common stressful situations for her to realize that even though stress was still high, she was better able to handle it and not over-react, and that her mood was more stable.

She also reported that even though she still woke up during the night, it was less often and she usually fell back asleep more easily. When we talked about what she had tried with the diet plan, and what was too hard about it, she realized that when she had followed it, she had fewer sugar cravings. I assured her that if she "ate all that food" she would actually be eating *fewer* calories because when she got over-hungry and binged on junk food, it was sabotaging all her efforts, and that NutraSweet was not only *not* a way to avoid the negative effects of the cycle, it actually made that cycle worse.

Over the next few months, we worked closely to customize the diet plan to her needs, while educating her about what she needed to do to nourish herself. It was a process of two steps forward, one step back, but her pain did continue to lessen, *and* she lost weight. These were big motivators to stick with it, even though none of it was happening as quickly as she would like (because she, of course, wanted it to change overnight and still worried that nothing would ever fully resolve the pain).

The breakthrough for her was when she stuck with the eating plan long enough to get to the point of being pain-free. Then she decided she didn't need to do it anymore, so she stopped… and her pain returned. A major breakthrough for people is when they realize their behaviors directly influence their symptoms, and that now they know how to avoid the symptoms they don't want. Even then, it is still a process of constantly finding the right balance, but now they are doing it because they have fully experienced the benefit and understand there are no other options, not because somebody told them to.

She still tended to worry about every little thing, but it no longer got the best of her. She could respond to what needed to be done, rather than just over-react and become paralyzed with anxiety and panic. She was sleeping through the night most nights, unless she deviated from her anti-inflammatory diet and either pain or increased anxiety worked her up. The anti-inflammatory diet was not just to help the physical symptoms, it also directly affected the inflammation in her brain which manifested as anxiety.

Not only did she feel better both physically and emotionally from dramatically better self-care, I was also able to convince her to start working with a therapist to address some of the family of origin issues with her mother that were now a daily struggle, as well as the negative patterns that had developed in her marriage.

She at first resisted this because she said she had "done lots of therapy, and talking about things doesn't actually change anything." But now that her mind was functioning at a much higher level, she was able to respond to therapy in a whole new way and found it very useful. Even her husband commented that he was more motivated to work with her "because it wasn't just the same old thing every time."

# Treating Bipolar Disorder

Chapter

## 20

- Is there adequate protein and nutrient intake?
- Are sleep and adrenal function being optimized?
- Is there female hormone imbalance?
- Is reactive hypoglycemia causing or exacerbating symptoms?
- Is the person engaging in physical movement?
- Is there essential fatty acid deficiency?
- Is there magnesium deficiency?
- Is there B-vitamin insufficiency?
- Is there neurosensitivity?
- Is vitamin D level optimized?

The diagnosis of bipolar disorder has expanded dramatically in recent years, with inclusion of additional subtypes of bipolar in the DSM-5, published by the American Psychiatric Association in 2013. Please see page 123 of the DSM-5 for the APA's summary of the differences among bipolar I disorder, bipolar II disorder, cyclothymic disorder, substance/medication-induced bipolar and related disorder, bipolar and related disorder due to another medical condition, other specified bipolar and related disorder, and unspecified bipolar and related disorder. The detailed criteria of each condition are then elaborated on in the rest of the section.

These additions have allowed many more people to recognize their symptoms within a diagnosis, but have also created a lot of misunderstanding about the nature of bipolar, what it means, and how to treat it. The expansion of the use of medications to treat bipolar into the primary care world has also led to greater confusion about what the diagnosis of bipolar really means, because patients quite often do not understand or even know which form of bipolar they have been diagnosed with. And, in my opinion, jumping to medication, all too often without thoroughly evaluating for all the functional medical conditions that result in bipolar symptoms, can prevent people from receiving the interventions that are most needed to stabilize and correct their conditions.

Regardless of which type of bipolar is being treated, applying the functional medicine technique of looking for the underlying imbalances and treating them will always be helpful. Sometimes, and more often in bipolar II, it can be curative. But even when it is not fully curative, these interventions can dramatically improve functioning, reduce suffering, and often help people require less medication.

With bipolar disorder, it is particularly difficult to prioritize the list of possible etiologies. There are always many involved, sometimes almost all are involved, and quite often different etiologies are primary at different stages of disease. These interactions cause the constantly changing state of bipolar disorder that makes it so difficult to fully understand and treat. The only way to fully address bipolar disorder is to address these issues simultaneously, to maximize overall stability of brain chemistry.

## Is There Adequate Protein and Nutrient Intake?

When brain chemistry is severely disrupted, such as in bipolar, normal eating patterns are often lost, leaving people even more vulnerable to sugar/carb addictions. This vulnerability is compounded by the fact that these are often the "easy" foods, which are readily available in prepared forms (things like candy and bread). People who generally feel poorly or unable to put together more complex foods often resort to these foods. Basic lack of nutrition creates both unsteady blood sugar and hormonal imbalances that then further disrupt neurochemistry, worsening the symptoms of bipolar. If the only treatment given is increased or new medication, this will not fix the problem and symptoms will continue to escalate.

The goal is to get people able to eat an anti-inflammatory diet, as well as to follow the guidelines to balance blood sugar. This may seem impossible when people are in crisis, but every step in the right direction helps. Educate about how what they do and do not eat changes brain chemistry and help them experience these changes for themselves. All too often, people get minimal help in this area and you may be the first person who gives them the tools and support they need to understand what they need to do in order to take care of their bodies and brains. Food will never be the quick fix to a crisis, but very often it is key to breaking out of the cycle of repeated crises.

Also check if acid blocking medications are being taken long-term. Protein pump inhibitors (PPIs) and H2 blockers are two different classes of medications that are used to treat heartburn, reflux, and GERD. They are available in both prescription and over-the-counter strengths. **Short-term use of these medications is safe, but long-term use can interfere with nutrient absorption leading to deficiencies in vitamins, minerals, and amino acids, all of which can contribute to bipolar depression.** The eating habits so many people with depression resort to contribute to digestive issues that these medications treat, but when the medications are used long-term, they can make both the digestive issues and mental/emotional symptoms worse.

Many people (but not all) who are self-treating with these medications will be able to wean off, simply by switching to a whole foods diet. Others will need additional support from functional medicine to fully heal. If a doctor (PCP or gastroenterologist) has prescribed any of these medications long-term, it is critical to work with a functional medicine doctor to ensure safety and long-term health.

**Action Items:**

1. *Ask patients if they are taking any of medications mentioned on the previous page, and if so, how long. If the person is struggling with discontinuing their over-the-counter self-medication or if their doctor has prescribed long-term use, refer to a functional medicine doctor.*

2. *Using tools from Chapters 7, 8, and 9, help people move towards eating a whole foods, anti-inflammatory diet. When people are struggling, break it into "baby steps." Every bit matters.*

3. *Focus on protein with every meal and snack.*

4. *Work not just with what people eat, but encourage them to eat frequently and on a consistent schedule.*

5. *Stick with it, repeatedly helping people overcome "I can't."*

## Are Sleep and Adrenal Function Being Optimized?

Many cases of bipolar II disorder are actually cases of adrenal dysregulation. When it gets severe enough, the volatility that adrenal dysregulation and blood sugar swings can cause will sometimes be called bipolar by doctors who do not recognize the signs of adrenal dysregulation. In these cases, adrenal support is the key to managing, and curing, bipolar.

In deeper cases of lifelong bipolar I disorder, adrenal support alone will not be sufficient, and ongoing management of the other factors will be necessary and will likely include pharmaceutical medications along with other therapies. But even if medications continue to be necessary, living with bipolar disorder is stressful, and the progressive effects of adrenal dysregulation due to that stress will exacerbate the bipolar symptoms. When symptoms worsen for this reason, simply increasing medication will typically make the person feel worse because it is not treating the real cause of the increased symptoms. Supporting adrenals can significantly improve stability and functioning, and help other therapies work more effectively. This can lower the need for medications, which can help people be more compliant because overall they feel much better. This is the synergistic response that integrated medicine can provide to help people break out of the downward spiral of suffering.

A key element to treating adrenal function in bipolar is eliminating caffeine. Caffeine use is extremely common in this population, and caffeine triggers both the highs and lows that get identified as bipolar swings. All too often, these swings are medicated, further contributing to the lethargy that pushes people to want more caffeine. Helping people break out of this cycle is a powerful way to help them feel better and often need less medication. This process is not easy for people who feel terrible both on and off medications, but the right education and support can help them achieve a whole new level of stability and functioning.

When people truly love their coffee or tea, switching to decaf is a way for them to enjoy the positive ritual that often develops around these beverages while eliminating the negative effects. Decaffeinated coffee and tea do contain tiny amounts of caffeine, but for the vast majority of people, it's not enough to cause problems.

**Action Items:**

1. *Initiate basic adrenal support:*
   - *adequate sleep*
   - *healthy meals*
   - *exercise*
   - *stress management techniques*
2. *Eliminate all forms of caffeine.*
3. *Consider referring to a functional medicine doctor or naturopath for more extensive adrenal support. This population often requires more than the basics to restore adrenal function, but an incorrect intervention can exacerbate bipolar, so expert help is recommended.*

## Is There Female Hormone Imbalance?

Female hormone imbalances are well known to cause mood disturbances and volatility in women and girls, but when the disturbances extend outside of the traditional PMS window, this aspect gets unrecognized and diagnosed as bipolar disorder. If bipolar is a new symptom around menopause, female hormones or other hormones (adrenal and thyroid) are the real cause of the issue.

Treating with birth control pills or hormone replacement therapy can be very helpful. However, if they are the only interventions used, the results are likely to be temporary or incomplete. Fully addressing female hormone imbalances requires examining the deeper relationship between female hormones, adrenal hormones, and thyroid hormones.

**Action Item:**

*If female hormone imbalance appears to be part of the problem, or even if it has already been identified as part of the problem, refer to functional or naturopathic medicine.*

## Is Reactive Hypoglycemia Causing or Exacerbating Symptoms?

Another extremely common cause of bipolar II disorder is nearly constant blood sugar swings. The mood volatility that results from blood sugar swings will sometimes be called bipolar by doctors who do not recognize the role blood sugar plays in mood. In these cases, stabilizing blood sugar is the key to managing, and curing, bipolar.

Even when blood sugar swings were not the initial cause of the bipolar swings, all too often people with bipolar tend to eat erratically, and eventually those habits result in blood sugar swings that exacerbate bipolar symptoms. As this issue develops, it very commonly looks as if a medication is losing its effectiveness. However, simply increasing medication, or trying a new medication, will typically make the person feel worse because what the person really needs is to stabilize their blood sugar.

For the summary of how reactive hypoglycemia can cause or contribute to the symptoms of bipolar disorder, return to Chapter 14 for the complete explanation of reactive hypoglycemia.

## Is the Person Engaging in Physical Movement?

Movement helps balance both the manic and the depressive phases of bipolar, so this is a population that requires strenuous exercise on a daily basis. For more information on how to address physical movement and how to use the various tools and strategies already discussed, revisit Chapter 6. For people suffering from bipolar, the emphasis needs to be on more strenuous forms of exercise.

## Is There Essential Fatty Acid Deficiency?

The most common fat deficiency in mental health disorders, particularly bipolar, depression, and ADHD, is lack of eicosapentaenoic acid (EPA) and docosahexaenoic acid (DHA). Restoring adequate EPA and DHA has been shown to reduce the symptoms of bipolar disorder. For a full overview of how essential fatty acids affect mental health, review the details in Chapter 8.

## Is There Magnesium Deficiency?

Because magnesium is necessary to relax, magnesium deficiency is a frequent cause of the volatility found in bipolar. Likely, it is not the only cause, because bipolar always has multiple contributing causes, but magnesium deficiency will make the symptoms worse.

To review how to evaluate if magnesium deficiency is contributing to bipolar, return to Chapter 13 for full assessment and treatment details.

## Is There B-Vitamin Insufficiency?

Different issues with B-vitamins can contribute to bipolar depression in different ways. Varying amounts of B-vitamin intake along with varying B-vitamin demand in the body due to variations in stress combine to make it unpredictable how someone will be feeling on a given day. During times of stress, especially if that stress is creating a more depressed response, making a concerted effort to consume extra B-vitamins will increase the chances that the body has the raw materials needed to effectively manage stress and stabilize mood, without causing mania.

Folic acid is an individual B-vitamin that needs to be evaluated in bipolar. People who have mutations in the MTHFR gene have a compromised ability to turn folic acid into its active form, called 5-MTHF. Lack of 5-MTHF can disrupt the production of multiple neurotransmitters, including serotonin, dopamine, and norepinephrine, all of which can contribute to bipolar symptoms. Refer to a psychiatrist who does MTHFR testing and appropriate treatment.

For full details on how to assess for B-vitamin sufficiency and how to treat if necessary, see Chapter 10.

### Action Items:

1. *Assess diet for daily intake of B-vitamins. Help people eat whole grains, beans, legumes, and nuts on a daily basis. Consider a B-complex supplement if intake is marginal or stress is very high.*

2. *When people are in the depressed phase of bipolar, or when stress is high and the response is depressive, consider a trial with a therapeutic dose of a B-complex supplement. (Do not consider this if the stress is creating a manic response.)*

3. *Refer to a psychiatrist who does MTHFR testing and treatment.*

## Is There Neurosensitivity to Chemicals?

People who suffer from bipolar disorder are much more likely to be among the people who have inflammatory reactions to one or more of the many chemicals that permeate our food supply and environment.

For a more information on how excess inflammation triggered by chemicals can impact mental health, see Chapter 16.

## Is Vitamin D Level Optimized?

Suboptimal vitamin D levels are extremely common and are correlated with higher rates of depression, including bipolar depression. Despite lack of research evaluating vitamin D treatment in bipolar depression, restoring vitamin D to optimal levels has been shown to improve depression and will not trigger mania. Correcting vitamin D will never be the full answer to balancing bipolar, but it is another factor that should not be overlooked.

Vitamin D is made when certain cells in the skin are exposed to ultraviolet light (sunlight). Therefore, the ways to increase vitamin D are through increased sun exposure or supplements. However, the risks associated with excess sun exposure (skin cancer, skin aging) are well known, and taking excess supplements can lead to vitamin D toxicity. The safest way to optimize vitamin D is to work with a doctor who will test and determine optimal vitamin D dosing for each individual to maintain long-term health.

### Action Item:

*Have patients work with their primary care physician to have vitamin D tested and maintained in the optimal range of 45 to 65ng/mL.*

## CASE STUDY
# Bipolar Disorder

Jason first came to my office seeking help with a recent diagnosis of diabetes. He was terrified of needles and didn't want to give himself insulin, even though his doctor had only recommended oral medication at that point.

As I started asking Jason about his eating habits, looking to discover why he had diabetes at age 28, he told me that he "sometimes ate well," but when he got stressed at work he would tend to drink a lot of coffee and binge on candy to keep his energy up, often pulling all-nighters.

He loved his job and got very excited talking about it, though he said sometimes the deadlines were very stressful, and that after he would work a couple weeks with very little sleep, he tended to crash. He would then spend a weekend alone in his apartment playing video games and sleeping. When it was really bad, he would even miss work for a while. He had lost a few jobs due to this, but he was also quite talented and his computer skills were in high demand, so he always managed to get another job.

When I asked him how long this had been going on, he said he had basically had this pattern since high school. It had been worst in college, when he had dropped out entirely, and his parents convinced him to see a doctor who diagnosed him with bipolar. He tried medication, but he said he didn't like how it made him feel, so he stopped it. This pattern repeated a few times during his college years, and even a few more times when he would get fired from a job he liked, but he said all the medicines just made him feel groggy and actually affected his work, so he would stop taking them.

He would do well for a while and make a lot of money, but then it always seemed to fall apart. Three times since college, he ended up living with his parents again—once after a divorce, once after overspending despite having a job, and once because he lost his job and had not saved enough to pay rent until he found another one.

At this point, I had no idea whether his bad habits were inducing a bipolar pattern or if he had an underlying bipolar that was inducing some of his bad habits. Either way, the key to helping both his physical and mental/emotional states was helping him understand that he needed to give himself the nutrition needed to fuel his brain, stabilize his blood sugar, and strengthen his adrenal function.

We started by helping him set a routine around both eating and sleeping. He said that he had never been a routine person, but I told him that curing his diabetes depended on giving his body what it needed, when it needed it. Even if his body didn't give him the signs, he had to be smarter than it.

He didn't like the idea of a meal plan, so the strategy was: three meals a day and each one had to contain at least 20 grams of protein and 10 grams of fiber. Ideally he would also avoid candy, bread, and other products made with refined sugar and flour, but the first priority was eating three meals a day, all containing protein, regardless of what else he ate. While it is best to keep sugar to a minimum, eating balanced meals regularly somewhat mitigates the negative effects of eating sugar. He also agreed to exercise on a daily basis and double up on exercise if he was craving sugar.

I also started him on fish oil because I wanted to help stabilize his mood to enable him to stick to the plan better, and since he didn't like fish, I knew eating fish alone wouldn't work quickly enough for him to really benefit before he was likely to experience more stress. Also, because his diet was so depleted, I started him on a high quality multi-vitamin to jump start his nutrition while he really figured out what the right diet was going to be for him.

Three weeks later, he was surprised at how much better he felt: His energy and his mood were more stable, and he found it easier to both fall asleep and get up in the morning. He still liked to stay up too late, so I further emphasized how important sleep is to balancing both blood sugar and mood. He said his mood was fine; that wasn't really the problem, but he was still concerned about his blood sugar.

Three months later, when we tested his blood sugar, he was no longer diabetic. I emphasized that if he continued to do what he was currently doing, the diabetes would stay resolved, but if he went back to his old habits, the diabetes would return again, and quickly. For several more months he did well, but then he disappeared for almost a year. When he came back, he was scared that the diabetes had returned. He said he had felt so good that it felt like he didn't need to do any of it anymore.

Sure enough, he had fallen back into his old pattern, and by the time he sought my help again, his diabetes had returned, so we restarted the same plan. And again, it worked: Three months later, his blood sugars had normalized. I again warned him about needing to stick with it, but the same thing happened again—he decided he felt so good, he didn't need any help from doctors. It actually took three rounds of this pattern for him to realize he really did have bipolar and that both his ups and downs were causing behaviors, which caused the diabetes.

At that point, he committed to seeing me every three months, whether he felt like he needed to or not, so we could discuss the current situation and make sure that he was as balanced as possible. He also agreed to start therapy to learn better skills for handling some of his work stress, so that he would not crash as low with his depressive episodes and not let his hypomania lead to poor self-care. After a year, we did take him off the multi-vitamin because he was generally sticking with a whole foods diet. We continued the fish oil because he didn't really like eating fish, and without it, I was concerned the bipolar would worsen and he would slide off the diet as well.

# Treating ADHD

- Is the person getting daily strenuous exercise?
- Is reactive hypoglycemia causing or exacerbating symptoms?
- Is there neurosensitivity to chemicals?
- Is there essential fatty acid deficiency?
- Is there magnesium deficiency?
- Is the person getting adequate amounts of refreshing sleep?

## Is the Person Getting Daily Strenuous Exercise?

Many Olympic athletes have related that they initially took up their sport to help with symptoms of ADHD. These are the most dramatic examples of how to turn ADHD into a strength rather than a weakness! People with ADHD are the portion of the population who require truly strenuous exercise on a nearly daily basis to thrive.

For a summary of how high-intensity activity (getting out of breath) has been shown to improve cognitive performance by changing neurotransmitters and hormones, review Chapter 6.

## Is Reactive Hypoglycemia Causing or Exacerbating Symptoms?

A significant portion of ADHD cases, particularly in children, are simply the result of blood sugar swings, and regulating blood sugar can cure the ADHD. Far too many children have rarely, if ever, eaten a healthy, balanced meal, and therefore their symptoms are continuous and often get labeled ADHD.

Even if blood sugar swings are not the initial cause of ADHD, people who suffer ADHD symptoms tend to eat irregularly, which causes blood sugar swings that mimic ADHD symptoms. Additionally, stimulant medication can further diminish the signals of hunger and exacerbate the blood sugar swings even more, which often results in worsening symptoms and higher doses of medications, which then further contribute to the vicious cycle.

For a summary of how reactive hypoglycemia can cause the symptoms of ADHD and what to do about it, review Chapter 14. For people with ADHD, using phone alarms to remind them to eat on schedule can be an invaluable tool to providing adequate protein and nutrient intake and training them how to optimally feed their brains.

## Is There Neurosensitivity to Chemicals?

People who suffer from ADHD are much more likely than the average population to react to one or more of the chemicals that are ubiquitous in the food supply and the environment. For a summary of these chemicals and how to avoid them, as well as for more detail on the inflammatory nature of these reactions, see chapter 16.

## Is There Essential Fatty Acid Deficiency?

Studies have shown that in many people with ADHD, replacing the deficient EPA and DHA has therapeutic benefit. Therefore, replenishing these commonly deficient essential fatty acids should be a first-line consideration in an overall treatment plan. Refer to Chapter 8 for the full discussion of essential fats.

## Is There Magnesium Deficiency?

Because magnesium is necessary to relax, magnesium deficiency is a frequent cause of the hyperactivity found in ADHD. Likely, it is not the only cause, because ADHD typically has multiple contributing factors, but magnesium deficiency will make the symptoms worse. Magnesium deficiency can also contribute to a wide variety of other health conditions, which cause pain and anxiety, further disrupting focus. For the summary of how to assess for magnesium deficiency and how to treat it, see Chapter 13.

## Is the Person Getting Adequate Amounts of Refreshing Sleep?

One of the many effects of inadequate or poor sleep is difficulty focusing and diminished executive function. Many people do not realize they are not getting adequate sleep, and therefore, do not identify it as a problem. Always ask about sleep amount and sleep quality, even when people do not complain about it. Help people experiment with getting more sleep if they are getting fewer than nine hours per night, or even more if they have been sleep-deprived.

More commonly, people with ADHD know they are struggling with sleep. They have difficulty falling asleep or staying asleep, sometimes because of stress and sometimes for no reason they can figure out. When people are struggling with difficulty sleeping, go back to the basics. Evaluate sleep environment and bedtime routine and help people make any necessary changes. Don't underestimate how powerful working with the basics can be: many people struggle deeply with these issues and you will likely be the first person to address them meaningfully.

If the person is consuming any form of caffeine (coffee, tea, energy drinks, soda, pills), evaluate the full effects the caffeine is having. Caffeine can improve focus for many people with ADHD, particularly in the short-term. However, it is still important to evaluate its longer-term effects and determine if it is contributing to sleep deprivation that is causing or exacerbating the ADHD symptoms. See Chapter 5 for the full discussion of sleep and debunking the caffeine myths.

**Action Item:**

*Work with the four fundamental components of sleep. Help people make sleep a priority and overcome the obstacles that interfere with quality sleep.*

## CASE STUDY
# Rose and ADHD

At age 46, Rose was diagnosed with ADHD. Her doctor prescribed Vyvanse and it changed her world: she was more organized at work and was even given a bonus for increased productivity. More importantly to her, she was less anxious in social situations because she followed conversations better and she felt like she was a better friend.

Sounds like the perfect result, so why did she end up in my office? Because despite those improvements, now she was irritable, even agitated sometimes, and lost her temper easily. She was having fights with her husband over things that they had never fought over before, and she didn't like it. Recently she had even snapped at one of her co-workers, and this had caused so much conflict at work that she decided taking the Vyvanse wasn't worth it. She stopped taking it and sought my help because she wanted to know if there was something that might help her the way the Vyvanse did, but without unwanted side effects.

As I gathered her medical history, it turned out this wasn't the only drug that had given her a mixed reaction. She knew caffeine helped her focus, but she had figured out that it made her wake up in the middle of the night, and more recently, had also started giving her hot flashes. She knew sleep was important for focus, and was frustrated that everything that helped also hurt in some way.

When I first started taking her case, I wasn't sure whether she had ADHD causing anxiety symptoms, or whether she had anxiety causing ADHD-like symptoms. But it quickly became clear that all of these issues were causing a lot of stress in her life, so I started with adrenal support. In her case, because the caffeine helped some, I kept her on the caffeine and used rhodiola, an adaptogen that is very helpful for improving focus. We also worked 164 Natural Treatments for Mental Health with her diet to make sure she was getting adequate B-vitamins and magnesium. Additionally, I started her on fish oil because she did not like eating fish and was allergic to nuts, which left her susceptible to deficiency of omega-3 fats.

Over the next six weeks, these changes helped some, but not nearly as much as Vyvanse. I was concerned that poor sleep was preventing her from really improving as much she could, so at that point, I did have her stop the coffee/caffeine and added in licorice for additional adrenal support during that time. These changes helped her sleep better, which she did like, but it didn't help her focus as much as either of us hoped.

That is when I suggested she go back on the Vyvanse. This surprised her, but my hope was that, after doing significant adrenal support, she might have a different reaction to the Vyvanse, meaning she would experience the positive effect without the negative effect. And this is exactly what happened: once again she was more organized at work and less anxious socially. But she did not experience the agitation and irritability—after doing the adrenal support, her body was better able to tolerate and respond to the medication, and she experienced the positive effects of the medication without the negative effects.

Because she was performing better overall and her mood was more stable, she felt less anxious than at any point in her life. By the time this happened, I was already convinced that her real issue was ADHD, and that her anxiety was a result of the symptoms of ADHD, not the other way around. (She wasn't diagnosed as a child because no one was diagnosed with ADHD during the time period she was a child.)

While I would love to say that if everyone did everything right, no one would need any medications; it is simply not true. This case is an example of the power of integrative medicine. When we take the true holistic approach to understand all the different factors involved and apply all the therapies that are necessary, this is how we help people achieve their highest level of health, functioning, and happiness. Sometimes integrative medicine success involves helping people experience the benefits of medications without the negative effects.

# Treating Irritability/Anger

---

- Is reactive hypoglycemia causing or exacerbating the symptoms?
- Does the person get adequate amounts of refreshing sleep?
- Is adrenal function being optimized?
- Is there female or male sex hormone imbalance?
- Is there magnesium deficiency?
- Is the person engaging in physical movement?
- Is there neurosensitivity to chemicals?
- Is there essential fatty acid deficiency?

---

## Is Reactive Hypoglycemia Causing or Exacerbating Symptoms?

When people experience "waves" of irritability, the first thing to assess is the role blood sugar is playing. In modern life, one can almost always find a stressor on which to blame the irritability, but when people have highly varying responses to common life stresses, and sometimes over-react significantly, the most likely reason for the variation is whether blood sugar was stable at that moment. See Chapter 14 for the full discussion on blood sugar.

## Does the Person Get Adequate Amounts of Refreshing Sleep?

One of the many effects, and often one of the first effects, of inadequate or poor quality sleep is irritability. Many people do not realize they are not getting adequate sleep, and therefore do not identify it as a problem. Always ask about sleep amount and sleep quality, even when people do not complain about it. Help people experiment with getting more sleep if they are getting less than nine hours per night, or even more if they have been sleep-deprived.

When people are struggling with difficulty sleeping, go back to the basics. Evaluate sleep environment and bedtime routine, and help people make any necessary changes. Don't underestimate how powerful working with the basics can be: many people struggle deeply with the basics and you will likely be the first person to address them meaningfully. Stress is almost always playing a role in irritability, as well as every form of sleep issue, so if the basics around sleep are not enough, also consider the next step: supporting adrenal function.

## Action Item:

*Work with the four fundamental components of sleep (see Chapter 5). Help people make sleep a priority and overcome the obstacles that interfere with quality sleep.*

- *Assess sleep environment for safety and comfort*
- *Correct physical and social issues that disrupt sleep*
- *Evaluate caffeine use*

# Is Adrenal Function Being Optimized?

Invariably, stressors play a role in irritability, but compromised adrenal function diminishes the ability to cope with stress and exacerbates overreactions. An irritable or angry overreaction then tends to increase the stress, and the way to stop the downward spiral is by supporting adrenal function.

Work with all the aspects of basic adrenal support: adequate sleep, eating regular meals, daily activity, and stress management techniques. If the person is consuming any form of caffeine (coffee, tea, energy drinks, soda, pills) educate them about the secondary effects of caffeine and debunk any myths they may believe. (See Chapter 5 and the Handout on p. 39 about caffeine.) Caffeine can exacerbate irritability and strain adrenals. It also contributes to sleep disturbance, which can further exacerbate the emotional volatility. Eliminating caffeine is a critical first step for treating irritability when the person also has trouble getting enough sleep. While people often feel they can't live without their caffeine, the opposite is typically true: they live far more comfortably and effectively when they experiment with using less or none.

When people truly love their coffee or tea, switching to decaf is a way for them to enjoy the positive ritual that often develops around these beverages while eliminating the negative effects. Decaffeinated coffee and tea do contain tiny amounts of caffeine, but for the vast majority of people, it's not enough to cause problems.

## Action Items:

1. *Initiate basic adrenal support:*
   - *adequate sleep*
   - *healthy meals*
   - *exercise*
   - *stress management techniques*
2. *Eliminate all forms of caffeine.*
3. *Consider more extensive adrenal support, with herbs like ashwagandha.*

## Is There Sex Hormone Imbalance? (Female or Male!)

Female hormone imbalances are well known to cause irritability, volatility, and other mood disturbances in women and girls, but it's not just the female hormones that can be an issue: Male hormone imbalance can also contribute to irritability. Fully addressing hormone balance, in both men and women, requires examining the deeper relationship between female hormones, adrenal hormones, and thyroid hormones. Treating with hormone replacement therapy (which in women includes birth control pills) can be helpful; however, if they are the only interventions used, the results are likely to be temporary or incomplete.

**Action Item:**

>   *If male or female hormone imbalance appears to be part of the problem, or even if it has already been identified as part of the problem, refer to functional or naturopathic medicine.*

## Is There Magnesium Deficiency?

Because magnesium is necessary to relax, magnesium deficiency is a frequent cause of irritability. Likely it is not the only cause, because irritability typically has multiple contributing causes, but magnesium deficiency will make the symptoms worse. Magnesium deficiency can also contribute to a wide variety of other health conditions that cause pain and anxiety, further triggering irritability.

See Chapter 13 for the full discussion of magnesium, including identifying and correcting magnesium deficiency.

## Is the Person Engaging in Physical Movement?

Movement directly and immediately improves mood and ability to handle stress, and excessive irritability and anger can be a direct result of not getting enough exercise to balance and mitigate these stress responses. Typically, people who suffer from irritability and anger will benefit most from more strenuous exercise. However, particularly for people who also suffer from fatigue, evaluate people's responses to exercise. If vigorous exercise makes the fatigue worse, then more calming, meditative forms of yoga or tai chi will often work better. Treat each person as an individual and help them figure out how they respond to different forms of exercise and determine the best form for them.

For the summary of how physical activity changes neurochemistry, along with action items, see Chapter 6 for the full discussion.

## Is There Neurosensitivity to Chemicals?

Certain chemicals that are now ubiquitous in the food supply can cause inflammatory reactions in some people, and people with irritability or anger management difficulties are more likely to be suffering these unpredictable reactions. See Chapter 16 for a summary of how these chemicals affect the brain and how to avoid them, as well as the full discussion on how inflammation affects the brain.

## Is There Essential Fatty Acid Deficiency?

While there are no studies of how essential fatty acids (EFAs) directly affect irritability and anger, these are symptoms that are sometimes the first signs of a deeper problem developing such as bipolar disorder, ADHD, or psychosis. All of these diseases have been shown to benefit from restoring EPA and DHA levels. Because EPA and DHA deficiencies are so common, evaluate for these deficiencies and help people prevent some of these more severe disorders by acting early.

See Chapter 8 for the summary and action items on essential fats and brain function, as well as the full discussion on fats and essential fatty acids.

## CASE STUDY
# Irritability/Anger

Isaac was referred to my office by a local therapist who specializes in working with children on the autism spectrum. Isaac's mother had sought her help after talking with a pediatrician about their mutual concerns about his speech delay, anti-social behavior (violent tantrums, refusal to interact with the family) and hyperactivity. He was only two and a half, and had not yet had any neuropsychological evaluation, but this therapist knew better than to wait for a formal diagnosis and immediately referred him to me to look for underlying issues that could be causing his behaviors and delaying his speech.

At the first visit, Isaac's mom brought her own mom along to help. I heard him in the waiting room long before I saw him, and when I did see him, he was racing from end to end. When he ran to my office, the first thing he did was jump on the scale with his entire little body, and then bolted to the other side of the room and climbed up on the table before anyone could stop him. He was completely unresponsive to any form of redirection or time-out, and even a video on a phone only kept him in one place briefly before he was off again, running, touching, and jumping. One of my early thoughts was, "This might be the most textbook case of ADHD I've ever seen; I fear for this kid's teachers and mom!"

Grandma did her best to keep Isaac (and my office) safe, while I asked Mom about Isaac's symptoms and medical history. She said this was worse than he sometimes was—he was tired because he hadn't taken a nap that day and that always made things worse. But it also wasn't as bad as it sometimes was—at his worst, Isaac would have five to 10 tantrums a day, lasting from a few minutes of crying and screaming to half an hour of hitting and kicking other people, and banging his own head on the floor. She was constantly apologizing for his behavior, and during the course of the office visit I watched many appropriate discipline techniques fail as Isaac just became more and more upset about being restricted to the kids' corner of the room, despite having a video to watch.

She knew sleep was an issue; every night was a battle to get him to sit still long enough to fall asleep. She said he would fall asleep very quickly once he stopped moving, but getting him to stop moving felt nearly impossible. Once he was asleep he did stay asleep, but would wake up early the next morning, even when he was awake past midnight. Mom had also done some reading about ADHD and behavior issues, and was trying to avoid sugar and gluten, though she admitted she really couldn't tell if this made any difference. She really didn't want to medicate her son, especially when everyone had different opinions about what was really wrong, yet no one could tell her why the issues were happening.

Isaac really had no physical symptoms. He almost never got sick, didn't have any known allergies, although he was sometimes slightly constipated (bowel movements would skip a day). His gestation and delivery had been without incident, and he had thrived as an infant.

At this point, I was quite sure the most immediate cause of Isaac's tantrums were blood sugar crashes. Sleep was probably playing a role too, but we started with food. I wanted to see if stabilizing his blood sugar would help him be calmer and more responsive, and potentially allow his language to develop more rapidly. Despite his mom being very dedicated to feeding him well, she was focusing on the wrong things. Avoiding sugar is always a good idea, but avoiding gluten can sometimes make the problem worse. Many of the gluten-free substitutes that are now available are actually higher glycemic index than their gluten-containing originals, and act more like sugar in the body.

Therefore, I had Mom switch focus to make sure that *every* time he ate, he ate protein, fat, and fiber. The other key was feeding him often. Every two hours at the minimum, and really, every chance she got. I also had her read labels to make sure she was avoiding any food colorings and food dyes that can also trigger these issues. If he got hold of a piece of candy here and there, it wasn't the end of the world, he was simply required to eat some protein and fat as well. We also focused on getting the right fats—more omega-3 fats from salmon and nuts. Because dairy was a big part of his diet, I also started him on a magnesium supplement to make sure his calcium and magnesium intake were in balance, and that he wasn't magnesium deficient.

About a month later when Isaac came back to my office, he still ran into the room, but then he sat down to watch his video. That lasted almost 10 minutes before he asked if he could have a glove. The time before he had simply torn half the gloves out of the box that was on the wall. After the first glove, he wanted more, and when he was told no, he got upset. But when his mom gave him a hug and showed him the coloring books that were in the office, the tears ended without escalating into a full tantrum. Mom reported that the tantrums were occurring much less often, and they seemed to end sooner if she fed him.

Getting Isaac to sleep was still difficult. To address this, we focused on making sure he had an outlet for his energy—that he could run and jump and truly race around until he was tired, for several hours a day, not just a 20-minute trip to the park. We also made sure he had a chance to run around after dinner and before bed. Even when eating well, Isaac was blessed with incredibly high energy, though our culture has somewhat decided to label this a curse. We talked about channeling the energy into something positive, whether it was ADHD or not, and helping Isaac learn to use his strengths in a positive way instead of seeing them as a negative.

The increased focus on physical outlets for Isaac helped him get to bed with less of a battle, which meant he got to bed earlier. Additional sleep also helped his tantrums to the point where they were almost non-existent. More importantly, when they did happen, Mom could now predict it. They would happen when he didn't eat when he needed to or if he ate a lot of sweets without any other foods. There was no longer any doubt about what Isaac needed to do to keep his blood sugar balanced, and what the consequences were of not having it balanced.

Over the next two years, Isaac's speech caught up to appropriate levels, and he is on track with early academic performance. His behavior in school is appropriate and his teachers describe him as enthusiastic and a joy to work with, and no one at the school has suggested the ADHD diagnosis his mother feared. I expect that getting enough activity will be a challenge for him within the school environment, but with the right support, he will be able to thrive. At the moment, he not only loves gymnastics but excels at it, and Isaac is full of exuberant strength and energy rather than rage, dysfunction, and what likely would have been multiple diagnoses.

# A Lifelong Journey

If there were any magic bullet solutions to ease the suffering of our patients, we would have found them already. Mental illness is both diverse and complex, and most people can benefit from many different interventions to optimize their health and happiness. But fundamentally, the brain is a physical organ, and it simply cannot work the way it is supposed to work without meeting the three vital physical needs: sleep, activity, and food. All of the more complex biochemical and physiological functions that determine how someone feels and thinks depend upon on these three needs being met.

These essential requirements may sound basic, but never underestimate just how powerful going back to the basics can be. Whenever your patients (or you!) are feeling overwhelmed by the complexity of symptoms and potential treatment options, start by going back to the basics. You may be surprised how often it is a breakthrough experience when people get the education, guidance, and support they need to truly understand their own needs and overcome all the various obstacles that manifest as "I can't."

For a huge number of people, this process can truly cure the suffering that gets labeled as mental illness. Not meeting these basic human needs inflicts a tremendous amount of mental and emotional suffering that is completely avoidable. Medications will never be the answer for these people and, all too often, make people feel worse instead of better.

However, for many other people, these treatments alone will not be enough. There will always be situations and circumstances where pharmaceutical medications, as well as other interventions, will be necessary and helpful. However, medications will *never* substitute for attending to the fundamental basics of sleep, activity, and food. When someone does get a complete and continuous response to medication, they should consider themselves lucky. But if they are still suffering, despite medication, then we need to look deeper.

Regardless of severity of disease and other complicating factors, always start by evaluating each person's sleep, activities, and food intake. Educate people about how imbalances in any of these areas negatively impact how they feel and how they think. Work with people to build a foundation of restorative sleep, starting with permission to sleep and then creating an environment that allows for sleep. Help people find activities they truly enjoy and can engage in with others—effectively deepening that enjoyment. Teach people the difference between real foods and processed foods, and how to not fall victim to sophisticated marketing. Only then can people figure out what is truly the ideal diet for them.

Most importantly, help people overcome the obstacles that are preventing them from optimal self-care. All of our patients are under stress, and every one of us has used the excuses, "I'm too stressed to eat right," and, "I'm too busy exercise." But our job is to help people reframe their own lives and understand that the higher the stress, the more important self-care becomes. And when people get the support they need, they can experience, often for the first time, just how much better they feel when they give their body what it needs. This breakthrough experience is the goal, because that is when people start to develop their own motivation and actually want to do it on their own.

Not only do they start to feel better from self-care, when people's brains are working better, they actually become more capable of responding more quickly and more deeply to all the powerful psychotherapy techniques also available. This synergistic effect increases their functioning and starts the upward trajectory, allowing people to blossom in ways they were never able to before. Not only is it possible to break people out of the typical downward spiral of mental illness, but by bringing together the best of all worlds of medicine, we can help people achieve a level of functioning and happiness they have never known before.

# References

American Psychiatric Association. (2013). *Diagnostic and statistical manual of mental disorders* (5th ed.). Washington, DC: Author.

Amminger, G. P., et al. (2015). Longer-term outcome in the prevention of psychotic disorders by the Vienna omega-3 study. *Nature Communications, 6,* 7934.

Assunção, M. L., Ferreira, H. S., dos Santos, A. F., Cabral, C. R., & Florêncio, T. M. (2009, Jul). Effects of dietary coconut oil on the biochemical and anthropometric profiles of women presenting abdominal obesity. *Lipids, 44*(7), 593-601.

Bartley, C. A., Hay, M., & Block, M. H. (2013, Aug). Meta-analysis: Aerobic exercise for the treatment of anxiety disorders. *Progress in Neuro-Psychopharmacology & Biological Psychiatry, 45,* 34-39.

D'Adamo, C. R., & Sahin, A. (2014, Winter). Soy foods and supplementation: A review of commonly perceived health benefits and risks. *Alternative Therapies in Health and Medicine, 20*(Suppl 1), 39-51.

Devalia, V., Hamilton, M. S., Molloy, A. M., & British Committee for Standards in Haematology. (2014, Aug). Guidelines for the diagnosis and treatment of cobalamin and folate disorders. *British Journal of Haematology, 166*(4), 496-513. doi: 10.1111/bjh.12959. Epub 2014 Jun 18.

Feranil, A. B., Duazo, P. L., Kuzawa, C. W., & Adair, L. S. (2011). Coconut oil is associated with a beneficial lipid profile in pre-menopausal women in the Philippines. *Asia Pacific Journal of Clinical Nutrition, 20*(2), 190-195.

Guo, W., Nazim, H., Liang, Z., & Yang, D. (2016, Apr). Magnesium deficiency in plants: An urgent problem. *The Crop Journal, 4*(2), 83-91. https://doi.org/10.1016/j.cj.2015.11.003.

Ismail, A. A. A., Ismail, Y., & Ismail, A. A. (2017, Sep 22), Chronic magnesium deficiency and human disease; time for reappraisal? *QJM.* doi: 10.1093/qjmed/hcx186. [Epub ahead of print].

Jayakody, K., Gunadasa, S., & Hosker, C. (2014, Feb). Exercise for anxiety disorders: Systematic review. *British Journal of Sports Medicine, 48*(3), 187-196.

Nagata, C., et al. (2014, Mar). Soy intake and breast cancer risk: An evaluation based on a systematic review of epidemiologic evidence among the Japanese population. *Japanese Journal of Clinical Oncology, 44*(3), 282-295. doi: 10.1093/jjco/hyt203. Epub 2014 Jan 22.

Ng, Q. X., Ho, C. Y. X., Chan, H. W., Yong, B. Z. J., & Yeo, W. S. (2017, Oct). Managing childhood and adolescent attention-deficit/hyperactivity disorder (ADHD) with exercise: A systematic review. *Complementary Therapies in Medicine, 34,* 123-128.

Pollan, M. (2007). *The omnivore's dilemma: A natural history of four meals.* London: Penguin Press.

Pollan, M. (2008). *In defense of food: An eater's manifesto.* New York: Penguin Books.

Pollan, M. (2009). *Food rules: An eater's manual.* New York: Penguin Books.

Rimer, J., et al. (2012, Jul 11). Exercise for depression. *The Cochrane Database of Systematic Reviews,* (7): CD004366. doi: 10.1002/14651858.CD004366.pub5.

Rosen, R. L, et al. (2017). Elevated C-reactive protein and posttraumatic stress pathology among survivors of the 9/11 World Trade Center attacks. *Journal of Psychiatric Research,* 89, 14-21. doi: 10.1016/j.jpsychires.2017.01.007. Epub 2017 Jan 16.

Sarris, J. (2017, Aug 25). Clinical use of nutraceuticals in the adjunctive treatment of depression in mood disorders. *Australia's Psychiatry,* 25(4), 369-372. doi: 10.1177/1039856216689533. Epub 2017 Jan 31.

Saunders, E. F., et. al. (2016, Oct). Omega-3 and omega-6 polyunsaturated fatty acids in bipolar disorder: A review of biomarker and treatment studies. *The Journal of Clinical Psychiatry,* 77(10), e1301-e1308.

Seaton, T., B. Welle, S. L., Warenko, M. K., & Campbell, R. G. (1986, Nov). Thermic effect of medium-chain and long-chain triglycerides in man. *The American Journal of Clinical Nutrition,* 44(5), 630-634.

Shaffer, J. A., et al. (2014, Apr). Vitamin D supplementation for depressive symptoms: A systematic review and meta-analysis of randomized controlled trials. *Psychosomatic Medicine,* 76(3), 190-196. doi: 10.1097/PSY.0000000000000044.

Sonuga-Barke, E. J., et al. (2013, Mar). Nonpharmacological interventions for ADHD: Systematic review and meta-analyses of randomized controlled trials of dietary and psychological treatments. *American Journal of Psychiatry,* 170(3), 275-289. doi: 10.1176/appi.ajp.2012.12070991.

St-Onge, M. P., Ross, R., Parsons, W. D., & Jones, P. J. (2003, Mar). Medium-chain triglycerides increase energy expenditure and decrease adiposity in overweight men. *Obesity Research,* 11(3), 395-402.

Vasquez, A., Manso, G., & Cannell, J. (2004, Sep-Oct). The clinical importance of vitamin D (cholecalciferol): A paradigm shift with implications for all healthcare providers. *Alternative Therapies in Health and Medicine,* 10(5), 28-36.

Wallerstedt., S. M., Fastbom, J., Linke, J., & Vitols, S. (2017, Jan). Long-term use of proton pump inhibitors and prevalence of disease- and drug-related reasons for gastroprotection-a cross-sectional population-based study. *Pharmacoepidemiology and Drug Safety,* 26(1), 9-16. doi: 10.1002/pds.4135. Epub 2016 Nov 16.

# Resources

Abraham, G. E., Schwartz, U. D., & Lubran, M. M. (1981). Effect of vitamin B6 on plasma and red blood cell magnesium levels in premenopausal women. *Annals of Clinical and Laboratory Science, 11*(4), 333-336.

Abraham, G. E. (1984). Nutrition and the premenstrual tension syndromes. *Journal of Applied Nutrition, 36*, 103-122.

Abraham, G. E., & Hargrove, J. T. (1980). Effect of vitamin B6 on premenstrual symptomatology in women with premenstrual tension syndrome: a double-blind crossover study. *Infertility, 3*, 155.

Abrantes, A. M., et al. (2012, Dec 1). Design and rationale for a randomized controlled trial testing the efficacy of aerobic exercise for patients with obsessive-compulsive disorder. *Mental Health Physicians Association, 5*(2), 155-165.

Abrantes, A. M., et al. (2009, Oct). Acute changes in obsessions and compulsions following moderate-intensity aerobic exercise among patients with obsessive-compulsive disorder. *Journal of Anxiety Disorders, 23*(7), 923-927.

Adams, P. W., et al. (1973, Apr 28). Effect of pyridoxine hydrochloride (vitamin B6) upon depression associated with oral contraceptives. *Lancet, 1*(7809), 899-904.

Akhondzadeh, S., Mohammadi, M. R., & Khademi, M. (2004, Apr 8). Zinc sulfate as an adjunct as an adjunct to methyl-phenidate for the treatment of attention deficit hyperactivity disorder in children: a double blind and randomized trial [ISRCTN64132371]. *BMC Psychiatry, 4*, 9.

Allison, J. R. (1945). The relation of hydrochloric acid and vitamin B complex deficiency in certain skin diseases. *Southern Medical Journal, 38*(4), 235-241.

Amminger, G. P., et al. (2010, Feb). Long-chain omega-3 fatty acids for indicated prevention of psychotic disorders: a randomized, placebo-controlled trial. *Archives of General Psychiatry, 67*(2), 146-154.

Ananth, J. V., Ban, T. A., & Lehmann, H. E. (1973, Oct). Potentiation of therapeutic effects of nicotinic acid by pyridoxine in chronic schizophrenics. *Canadian Psychiatric Association Journal, (18)*, 377-383.

Arnold, L. E., Christopher, J., Huestis, R. D., & Smeltzer, D. J. (1978, Dec 8). Megavitamins for minimal brain dysfunction: a placebo-controlled study. *JAMA; 240*(24), 2642-2643.

Arnold, L. E., Young, A. S., Belury, M. A., Cole, R. M., Gracious, B., Seidenfeld, A. M., Wolfson, H., & Fristad, M. A. (2017, Apr). Omega-3 fatty acid plasma levels before and after supplementation: Correlations with mood and clinical outcomes in the omega-3 and therapy studies. *Journal of Child and Adolescent Psychopharmacology, 27*(3), 223-233.

Baisier, W.V., Hertoghe, J., & Eeckhaut, W. (2000). Thyroid insufficiency: is TSH measurement the only diagnostic tool?

*Journal of Nutrition & Environmental Medicine, 10*, 105-113.

Baker, H., Frank, O., & Jaslow, S. P. (1980, Jan). Oral versus intramuscular vitamin supplementation for hypovitaminosis in the elderly. *Journal of the American Geriatrics Society, 28*(1), 42-45.

Barnes, B. O., & Galton, L. (1976). *Hypothyroidism: The unsuspected illness.* New York, NY: Harper.

Barr, W. (1984, Apr). Pyridoxine supplements in the premenstrual syndrome. *Practitioner, 228*(1390), 425-427.

Barrie, S. A., et al. (1987, Jun). Comparative absorption of zinc picolinate, zinc citrate and zinc gluconate in humans. *Agents Actions, 21*(1-2), 223-228.

Bateman, B., et al. (2004). The effects of a double-blind, placebo controlled, artificial food colourings and benzoate preservative challenge on hyperactivity in a general population sample of preschool children. *Archives of Disease in Childhood, 89*(6), 506-511.

Benedict, C. R., Anderson, G. H., & Sole, M. J. (1983, Sep). The influence of oral tyrosine and tryptophan feeding on plasma catecholamines in man. *The American Journal of Clinical Nutrition, 38*(3), 429-435.

Benjamin, J., et al. (1995, Jul). Double-blind, placebo-controlled, crossover trial of inositol treatment for panic disorder. *American Journal of Psychiatry, 152*(7), 1084-1086.

Benkelfat, C., et al. (1994). Mood-lowering effect of tryptophan depletion. *Archives of General Psychiatry, 51*(9), 687-697.

Benzing, V., & Schmidt, M. (2017). Cognitively and physically demanding exergaming to improve executive functions of children with attention deficit hyperactivity disorder: A randomised clinical trial. *BMC Pediatrics, 17*(1), 8.

Berk, M., et al. (2008, Sep 15). N-Acetyl cysteine for depressive symptoms in bipolar disorder—a double-blind randomized placebo-controlled trial. *Biological Psychiatry, 64*(6), 468-475.

Berwid, O. G., & Halperin, J. M. (2012, Oct). Emerging support for a role of exercise in attention-deficit/hyperactivity disorder intervention planning. *Current Psychiatry Report, 14*(5), 543-51.

Bo-Linn, G. W., et al. (1984, Mar). An evaluation of the importance of gastric acid secretion in the absorption of dietary calcium. *Journal of Clinical Investigation, 73*(3), 640-647.

Bonnet, M. H., & Arand, D. L. (1996, Jul). The consequences of a week of insomnia. *Sleep, 19*(6), 453-461.

Boris, M., & Mandel, F. S. (1994, May). Foods and additives are common cause of the attention deficit hyperactive disorder in children. *Annals of Allergy, Asthma & Immunology, 72*(5), 462-468.

Boulenger, J. P., & Uhde, T. W. (1982, Oct). Caffeine consumption and anxiety: Preliminary results of a survey comparing patients with anxiety disorders and normal controls. *Psychopharmacology Bulletin, 18*(4), 53-57.

Boulenger, J. P., et al. (1984, Nov). Increased sensitivity to caffeine in patients with panic disorder. *Archives of General Psychiatry, 41*(11), 1067-1071.

Boyd, N. F., et al. (1988, Jul 16). Effect of a low-fat high carbohydrate diet on symptoms of cyclical mastopathy. *Lancet, 332*(8603), 128-132.

Bradley, J. R., & Petree, A. (1990). Caffeine consumption, expectancies of caffeine-enhanced performance, and caffeinism symptoms among university students. *Journal of Drug Education, 20*(4), 319-328.

Brayshaw, N. D., & Brayshaw, D. D. (1986, Dec 4). Thyroid hypofunction in premenstrual syndrome. *New England Journal of Medicine, 315*(23), 1486-1487.

Brenner, A. (1982, May). The effects of megadoses of selected B complex vitamins on children with hyperkinesis: controlled studies with long term followup. *Journal of Learning Disabilities, 15*(5), 258-264.

Brent, G. A. (1994, Sep 29). The molecular basis of thyroid hormone action. *The New England Journal of Medicine, 331*(13), 847-853.

Brooks, S. C., D'Angelo, L., Chalmeta, A., Ahern, G., & Judson, J. H. (1983, Nov). Pyridoxine and schizophrenic illness responsive to pyridoxine HCI (B6) subsequent to phenothiazine and butyrophenone toxicities. *Biological Psychiatry, 18*(11), 1321-1328.

Bruce, M., Scott, N., Shine, P., & Lader, M. (1992, Nov). Anxiogenic effects of caffeine in patients with anxiety disorders. *Archives of General Psychiatry, 49*(11), 867-869.

Bruni, O., Ferri, R., Miano, S., & Verillo, E., (2004 Jul). L-5-Hydroxytryptophan treatment of sleep terrors in children. *European Journal of Pediatrics, 163*(7), 402-407.

Brush, M. G., Watson, S. J., Horrobin, D. F., & Manku, M. S. (1984, Oct 15). Abnormal essential fatty acid levels in plasma of women with premenstrual syndrome. *American Journal of Obstetrics and Gynecology, 150*(4), 363-366.

Brush, M. G., Bennett, T., & Hansen, K. (1988, Nov). Pyridoxine in the treatment of premenstrual syndrome: A retrospective survey in 603 patients. *British Journal of Clinical Practice, 42*(11). 448-452.

Buist, R. A. (1983). The therapeutic predictability of tryptophan and tyrosine in the treatment of depression. *International Clinical Nutrition Review, 3*(2), 1-3.

Bunevicius, R., Kazanavicius, G., Zalinkevicius, R. & Prange, Jr., A. J. (1999, Feb 11). Effects of thyroxine as compared with thyroxine plus triiodothyronine in patients with hypothyroidism. *New England Journal of Medicine, 340*(6), 424-429.

Cameron, O. G., & Nesse, R. M. (1988). Systemic hormonal and physiological correlations in anxiety disorder. *Psychoneuroendocrinology, 13*(4), 287-307.

Campbell, M., et al. (1973, Nov). Liothyronine treatment in psychotic and nonpsychotic children under 6 years. *Archives of General Psychiatry, 26*(5), 602-608.

Capper, W. M., et al. (1967, Feb 25). Gallstones, gastric secretion and flatulent dyspepsia. *Lancet, 1*(7487), 413-415.

Charney, D. S., Heninger, G. R., & Jarlow, P. I. (1985, Mar). Increased anxiogenic effects of caffeine in panic disorders. *Archives of General Psychiatry, 42*(3), 233-43.

Chou, C. C., & Huang, C. J. (2017, Jan 12). Effects of an 8-week yoga program on sustained attention and discrimination function in children with attention deficit hyperactivity disorder. *PeerJ, 5*, e2883.

Chouinard, G., Young, S. N., Annable, L., & Sourkes, T. L. (1977, Jan 29). Tryptophan-nicotinamide combination in depression. *Lancet, 1*(8005), 249.

Chouinard, G., Young, S. N., Annable, L., & Sourkes, T. L. (1979, Apr). Tryptophan-nicotinamide, imipramine and their combination in depression. *Acta Psychiatrica Scandinavica, 59*(4), 395-414.

Coleman, M., et al. (1976). The role of whole blood serotonin levels in monitoring vitamin B6 and drug therapy in hyperactive children. *Monographs in Neural Science, 3*, 133-136.

Coleman, M., et al. (1979, Oct). A preliminary study of the effect of pyridoxine administration in a subgroup of hyperkinetic children: a double-blind crossover comparison with methylphenidate. *Biological Psychiatry, 14*(5), 741-751.

Colquhoun, I., & Bunday, S. (1981, May). A lack of essential fatty acids as a possible cause of hyperactivity in children. *Medical Hypotheses, 7*(5), 673-679.

Conners, C. K., et al. (1976, Aug). Food additives and hyperkinesis: a controlled double-blind experiment. *Pediatrics, 58*(2). 154-166.

Conners, C. K., Goyette, C. H., & Newman, E. B. (1980, Nov). Dose-time effect of artificial colors in hyperactive children. *Journal of Learning Disabilities, 13*(9), 512-516.

Cook, J. D., Morck, T. A., & Lynch, S. R. (1981, Dec). The inhibitory effect of soy products on nonheme iron absorption in man. *The American Journal of Clinical Nutrition, 34*(12), 2622-2629.

Coppen, A., & Bailey, J. (2000, Nov). Enhancement of the antidepressant action of fluoxetine by folic acid: a randomized, placebo controlled trial. *Journal of Affective Disorders, 60*(2), 121-130.

Council on Drugs. (1963). New drugs and developments in therapeutics. *JAMA, 183*, 362.

Cowdry, R. W., Wehr, T. A., Zis, A. P., & Goodwin, F. K. (1983, Apr). Thyroid abnormalities associated with rapid-cycling bipolar illness. *Archives of General Psychiatry, 40*(4), 414-420.

Crook, W. G., et al. (1961, May). Systemic manifestation due to allergy. Report of fifty patients and a review of the literature on the subject (sometimes referred to as allergic toxemia and the allergic tension-fatigue syndrome). *Pediatrics, 27*, 790-799.

Crook, W. G. (1980, May). Can what a child eats make him dull, stupid, or hyperactive? *Journal of Learning Disabilities, 13*(5), 281-286.

Crowley, T. J., Chesluk, D., Dilts, S., et al., (1974). Drug and alcohol abuse among psychiatric admissions—multidrug clinical-toxicology study. *Archives of General Psychiatry, 30*, 13-20.

Cuskelly, G. J., McNulty, H., & Scott, J. M. (1996, Mar 9). Effect of increasing dietary folate of red-cell folate: Implications for prevention of neural tube defects. *Lancet, 347*(9002), 657-59.

Davidson, J. R., Abraham, K., Connor, K. M., & McLeod, M. N. (2003, Feb). Effectiveness of chromium in atypical depression: A placebo-controlled trial. *Biological Psychiatry, 53*(3), 261-264.

Daynes, G. (1975, Aug 9). Letter: Cyanocobalamin in postpartum psychosis. *South African Medical Journal, 49*(34), 1373.

De Freitas, B., & Schwartz, G. (1979, Oct). Effects of caffeine in chronic psychiatric patients. *American Journal of Psychiatry, 136*(10), 1337-1338.

Dekker, D. K., Paley, M. J., Popkin, S. M., & Tepas, D. I. (1993, Jan-Mar). Locomotive engineers and their spouses: Coffee consumption, mood, and sleep reports. *Ergonomics, 36*(1-3), 233-38.

Deutch, B., Jorgensen, E. B., & Hansen, J. C. (2000). Menstrual discomfort in Danish women reduced by dietary supplements of omega-3 PUFA and B12 (fish oil or seal oil capsules). *Nutrition Research, 20*, 621-631.

Docherty, J. P., et al. (2005, Sep). A double-blind, placebo-controlled, exploratory trial of chromium picolinate in atypical depression: Effect on carbohydrate craving. *Journal of Psychiatric Practice, 11*(5), 302-314.

Dodd, S., et al. (2013, Apr 5). Putative neuroprotective agents in neuropsychiatric disorders. *Prog Neuropsychopharmacol Biological Psychiatry, 42*, 135-45.

Dotevall, G., & Walan, A. (1969, Jan-Dec). Gastric secretion of acid and intrinsic factor patients with hyper- and hypothyroidism. *Acta Medica Scandinavica, 186*(1-6), 529-533.

Downing, D. (2000). Hypothyroidism: Treating the patient not the laboratory. *Journal of Nutritional & Environmental Medicine, 10*, 101-103.

Dutta, S. K., Bustin, M. P., Russell, R. M., & Costa, B. S. (1982, Oct). Deficiency of fat soluble vitamins in treated patients with pancreatic insufficiency. *Annals of Internal Medicine, 97*(4), 549-552.

Egger, J., et al. (1985, Mar 9). Controlled trial of the oligoantigenic treatment in the hyperkinetic syndrome. *Lancet, 1*(8428), 540-545.

Ellis, F. R., & Nasser, S. (1973, Sep). A pilot study of vitamin B12 in the treatment of tiredness. *British Journal of Nutrition, 30*(2), 277-283.

Elwes, R. D., et al. (1989, Nov 4). Treatment of narcolepsy with L-tyrosine: Double-blind placebo-controlled trial. *Lancet, 2*(8671), 1067-1069.

Emsley, R., Myburgh, C., Oosthuizen, P., & van Rensburg, S. J. (2002). Randomized, placebo-controlled pilot study of ethyl-eicosapentaenoic acid as supplemental treatment in schizophrenia. *American Journal of Psychiatry, 159*(9), 1596-1598.

Evans, D. L., Edelsohn, G. A., & Golden, R. N. (1983, Feb). Organic psychosis without anemia or spinal cord symptoms in patients with vitamin B12 deficiency. *American Journal of Psychiatry, 140*(2), 218-221.

Facchinetti, F., et al. (1991, Aug). Oral magnesium successfully relieves premenstrual mood changes. *Obstetrics and Gynecology, 78*(2), 177-181.

Feldmesser Reiss, E. E. (1958, Dec). The application of triiodothyronine in the treatment of mental disorders. *Journal of Nervous and Mental Disease, 127*(6), 540-545.

Fenton, W. S., et al. (2001, Dec). A placebo-controlled trial of omega-3 fatty acid (ethyl eicosapentaenoic acid) supplementation for residual symptoms and cognitive impairment in schizophrenia. *American Journal of Psychiatry, 158*(12), 2071-2074.

Field, R. (1993, Apr 8). Melatonin may relieve sleep-cycle disorders. *Medical Tribune, 2.*

Fitten, L. J., Profita, J. & Bidder, T. G. (1985, Apr). L-tryptophan as a hypnotic in special patients. *Journal of the American Geriatrics Society, 33*(4), 294-297.

Frangou, S., Lewis, M., & McCrone, P. (2006, Jan). Efficacy of ethyl-eicosapentaenoic acid in bipolar depression; randomized double-blind placebo-controlled study. *British Journal of Psychiatry, 188*, 46-50.

Frank, O., et al. (1977). Superiority of periodic intramuscular vitamin injections over daily oral vitamins in maintaining normal vitamin titers in a geriatric population. *The American Journal of Clinical Nutrition, 30*, 630.

Fredrikson, H. (1946). The role of the thyroid in certain menstrual disorders. *Acta Obstetricia et Gynecologica Scandinavica, 26*(1). 11-40.

Freeman, M. P., et al. (2006, Jan). Randomized dose-ranging pilot trial of omega-3 fatty acids for postpartum depression. *Acta Psychiatrica Scandinavica, 113*(1), 31-35.

Fux, M., Levine, J., Aviv, A., & Belmaker, R. H. (1996, Sep). Inositol treatment of obsessive-compulsive disorder. *American Journal of Psychiatry, 153*(9), 1219-1221.

Gaby, A. R. (2004, Jun). Sub-laboratory hypothyroidism and the empirical use of Armour thyroid. *Alternative Medicine Review, 9*(2), 157-179.

Garfinkel, D., Laudon, M., Nof, D., & Zisapel, N. (1995, Aug 26). Improvement of sleep quality in elderly people by controlled-release melatonin. *Lancet, 346*(8974), 541-544.

Garfinkel, D, Zisapel, N., Wainstein, J., & Laudon, M. (1999, Nov 8). Facilitation of benzodiazepine discontinuation by melatonin: A new clinical approach. *Archives of Internal Medicine, 159*(20), 2456-2460.

Gelenberg, A. J., et al. (1980). Tyrosine for the treatment of depression. *American Journal of Psychiatry, 137*(5), 622-623.

Gesch, C. B., et al. (2002, Jul). Influence of supplementary vitamins, minerals, and essential fatty acids on the antisocial behavior of young adult prisoners. Randomised, placebo-controlled trial. *British Journal of Psychiatry, 181,* 22-28.

Gilliland, R., & Andress. D. (1981, Apr). Ad lib caffeine consumption, symptoms of caffeinism, and academic performance. *American Journal of Clinical Psychiatry, 138*(4), 512-14.

Godfrey, P.S., et al. (1990, Aug 18). Enhancement of recovery from psychiatric illness by methylfolate. *Lancet, 336*(8712), 392-395.

Goggans, F. C. (1984, Feb). A case of mania secondary to vitamin B12 deficiency. *American Journal of Psychiatry, 141*(2). 300-301.

Gold, M. S., Pottash, A. L., & Extein, I. (1981, May 15). Hypothyroidism and depression. Evidence from complete thyroid function evaluation. *JAMA, 245*(19), 1919-1922.

Goldberg, I. K. (1980, Aug 16). L-tyrosine in depression. *Lancet, 2*(8190), 364-365.

Golding, D. N. (1970, Jan). Hypothyroidism presenting with musculoskeletal symptoms. *Annals of the Rheumatic Diseases, 29*(1), 10-14.

Goodwin, F. K., et al. (1982, Jan). Potentiation of antidepressant effects by L-triiodothyronine in tricyclic nonresponders. *American Journal of Psychiatry, 139*(1), 34-38.

Gorman, J. M., & Liebowitz, M. R. (1985). Panic and anxiety disorders. In R. Michels et al. (Eds.), *Psychiatry, vol. 1* (pp. 1-13). Philadelphia: J. B. Lippincott.

Greden, J. F. (1974, Oct). Anxiety or caffeinism: A diagnostic dilemma. *American Journal of Psychiatry, 131*(10),1089-1092.

Green, A. R., & Curzon, G. (1970, Jun). The effect of tryptophan metabolites on brain 5-hydroxytryptamine metabolism. *Biochemical Pharmacology, 19*(6), 2061-2068.

Grenyer, B. F., et al. (2007, Oct). Fish oil supplementation in the treatment of major depression: A randomized double-blind placebo controlled trial. *Progress in Neuro-Psychopharmacology & Biological Psychiatry, 31*(7), 1393-1396.

Hagen, I., Nesheim, B. I, & Tuntland, T. (1985). No effect of vitamin B-6 against premenstrual tension. *Acta Obstetricia et Gynecologica Scandinavica, 64*(8), 667-670.

Hallert, C., Aström, J., & Walan, A. (1983, Mar). Reversal of psychopathology in adult celiac disease with the aid of pyridoxine (vitamin B6). *Scandinavian Journal of Gastroenterology, 18*(2), 299-304.

Harel, Z., Biro, F. M., Kottenhahn, R. K., & Rosenthal, S.L. (1996, Apr). Supplementation with omega-3 polyunsaturated fatty acids in the management of dysmenorrhea in adolescents. *American Journal of Obstetrics and Gynecology, 174*(4), 1335-1338.

Harley, J. P., et al. (1978, June). Hyperkinesis and food additives: Testing the Feingold hypothesis. *Pediatrics, 61*(6), 818-828.

Hartmann, E. (1977, Apr). L-tryptophan: A rational hypnotic with clinical potential. *American Journal of Psychiatry, 134*(4), 336-370.

Hermesh, H., Weizman, A., Shahar, A., & Munitz, H. (1988, Jul). Vitamin B12 and folic acid serum levels in obsessive compulsive disorder. *Acta Psychiatrica Scandinavica, 78*(1), 8-10.

Hoffer, A. (1972, Jul 22). Treatment of hyperkinetic children with nicotinamide and pyridoxine. *Canadian Medical Association Journal, 107*(2), 111-112.

Hoffer, A., & Osmond, H. (1963, May). Scurvy and schizophrenia. *Dis Nervous System, 24,* 273-285.

Horrobin, D. F., & Manku, M. S. (1989, Sep). Premenstrual syndrome and premenstrual breast pain (cyclical mastalgia): Disorders of essential fatty acid (EFA) metabolism. *Prostaglandins Leukot Essential Fatty Acids, 37*(4), 255-261.

Howard III, J. S. (1975, Jul). Folate deficiency in psychiatric practice. *Psychosomatics, 16*(3), 112-115.

Hoza, B., Martin, C. P., Pirog, A., & Shoulberg, E. K. (2016, Dec). Using physical activity to manage ADHD symptoms: The state of the evidence. *Current Psychiatry Reports, 18*(12), 113.

Hughes, E. C., et al. (1982, Nov). Food sensitivity in attention deficit disorder with hyperactivity (ADD/HA): A procedure for differential diagnosis. *Annals of Allergy, Asthma & Immunology, 49*(5), 276-280.

Hughes, G. V., & Boland, F. J. (1992, Sep-Oct). The effects of caffeine and nicotine consumption on mood and somatic variables in a penitentiary inmate population. *Addictive Behaviors, 17*(5), 447-457.

Hughes, J. R, Higgins, S. T., Bickel, W. K., et al., (1991, Jul). Caffeine self-administration, withdrawal, and adverse effects among coffee drinkers. *Archives of General Psychiatry, 48*(7), 611-617.

Hullet, F. J., & Bidder, T. G. (1983, May). Phenelzine plus triiodothyronine combination in a case of refractory depression. *Journal of Nervous and Mental Disease, 171*(5), 318-320.

Hung, C. L., Huang, C. J., Tsai, Y. J., Chang, Y. K., & Hung, T. M. (2016, Oct 13). Neuroelectric and behavioral effects of acute exercise on task switching in children with attention-deficit/hyperactivity disorder. *Frontiers in Psychology, 7*, 1589.

Iancu, I., Dolberg, O. T., & Zohar, J. (1996, Apr). Is caffeine involved in the pathogenesis of combat-stress reaction? *Military Medicine, 161*(4), 230-232.

Israëls, M. C., & Simmons, A. V. (1967). Ferrous sulfate with ascorbic acid in iron-deficiency anemia. *Lancet, 1*, 1297-1299.

Kahn, R. S., & Westenberg, H. G. (1985, Mar-Apr). L-5 Hydroxytryptophan in the treatment of anxiety disorders. *Journal of Affective Disorders, 8*(2), 197-200.

Kanofsky, J. D., et al. (1989). Ascorbate: An adjunctive treatment for schizophrenia. *The Journal of the American College of Nutrition, 8*(5), 425.

Kaplan, B. J., McNicol, J., Conte, R. A., & Moghadam, H. K. (1989, Jan). Dietary replacement in preschool-aged hyperactive boys. *Pediatrics, 83*(1), 7-17.

Kaplan, B. J., et al. (2001, Dec). Effective mood stabilization with chelated mineral supplement: An open label trial in bipolar disorder. *The Journal of Clinical Psychiatry, 62*(12), 936-944.

Karlan, S. C., & Cohn, C. (1946, Mar 2). Hypoglycemic fatigue. *JAMA, 130*, 553-555.

Kendall, K. E., & Schnurr, P. P. (1987, Aug). The effects if vitamin B6 supplementation in premenstrual symptoms. *Obstetrics and Gynecology, 70*(2), 145-149.

Kershner, J., & Hawke, W. (1979, May). Megavitamins and learning disorders: A controlled double-blind experiment. *Journal of Nutrition, 109*(5), 819-826.

Khoo, S. K., Munro, C., & Battistutta, D. (1990, Aug). Evening primrose oil and treatment if premenstrual syndrome. *Medical Journal, 153*(4), 189-192.

King, D. S. (1981, Jan). Can allergic exposure provoke psychological symptoms? A double-blind test. *Biological Psychiatry, 16*(1), 3-19.

Koczapski, A., Paredes, J., Kogan, C., Ledwidge, B., & Higenbottam, J. (1989). Effects of caffeine on behavior of schizophrenic inpatients. *Schizophrenia Bulletin, 15*(2) 339-344.

Konofal, E., Lecendreux, M., Armulf, I., & Mouren, M. C. (2004, Dec). Iron deficiency in children with attention-deficit/hyperactivity disorder. *Archives of Pediatrics & Adolescent Medicine, 158*(12), 1113-1115.

Konofal, E., Cortese, S., Lecendreux, M., Armulf, I., & Mouren, M. C. (2005, Nov). Effectiveness of iron supplementation in a young child with attention-deficit/hyperactivity disorder. *Pediatrics, 116*(5), e732-e734.

Konofal, E., Lecendreux, M., Deron, J., Marchand, M., Cortese, S., Zaïm, M., Mouren, M. C., Arnulf, I. (2008, Jan). Effects of iron supplementation on attention deficit hyperactivity disorder in children. *Pediatric Neurology, 38*(1), 20-26.

Krugman, L. G., et al. (1975, Jul). Patterns of recovery of the hypothalamic-pituitary-thyroid axis in patients taken off chronic thyroid therapy. *The Journal of Clinical Endocrinology and Metabolism, 41*(1), 70-80.

Lafleur, D. L., et al. (2006, Jan). N-acetylcysteine augmentation in serotonin reuptake inhibitor refractory obsessive-compulsive disorder. *Psychopharmacology, 184*(2), 254-256.

Lane, J. D., Adcock, R. A., Williams, R. B., & Kuhn, C. M. (1990, May-Jun). Caffeine effects on cardiovascular and neuroendocrine responses to acute psychosocial stress and their relationship to level of habitual caffeine consumption. *Psychosomatic Medicine, 52*(3), 320-36.

Lane, J. D. (1997, Sep). Effects of brief caffeinated-beverage deprivation on mood, symptoms, and psychomotor performance. *Pharmacology, Biochemistry and Behavior, 58*(1), 203-208.

Lansdowne, A. T, & Provost, S. C. (1998, Feb). Vitamin D3 enhances mood in healthy subjects during winter. *Psychopharmacology, 135*(4), 319-323.

Larsson, B., Jonasson, A., & Fianu., S. (1989). Evening primrose oil in the treatment of premenstrual syndrome: A pilot study. *Current Therapeutic Research, 46*, 58-63.

Laugharne, J. D., Mellor, J. E., & Peet, M. (1996, Mar). Fatty acids and schizophrenia. *Lipids, 31*(Suppl), S163-S165.

Lee, M. A., Flegel, P., Greden, J. F., & Cameron, O. G. (1988, May). Anxiogenic effects of caffeine on panic and depressed patients. *American Journal of Psychiatry, 145*(5), 632-635.

Leibenluft, E., Fiero, P. L., Bartko, J. J., Moul, D. E., & Rosenthal, N. E. (1993, Feb). Depressive symptoms and the self-reported use of alcohol, caffeine, and carbohydrates in normal volunteers and four groups of psychiatric outpatients. *American Journal of Psychiatry, 150*(2), 294-301.

Levy, F., et al. (1978, Jan 28). Hyperkinesis and diet: A double-blind crossover trial with a tartrazine challenge. *Medical Journal Australia, 1*(2), 61-64.

Lewis, J. E., et al. (2013, Jan 21). The effect of methylated vitamin B complex on depressive and anxiety symptoms and quality of life in adults with depression. *ISRN Psychiatry, Article ID 621453.* doi: 10.1155/2013/621453.

Lindberg, D., et al. (1979, Sep). Symptom reduction in depression after treatment with L-tryptophan or imipramine. *Acta Psychiatrica Scandinavica, 60*(3), 287-294.

Lindenbaum, J., et al. (1988, June 30). Neuropsychiatric disorders cause by cobalamin deficiency in the absence of anemia or macrocytosis. *The New England Journal of Medicine, 318*(26), 1720-1728.

Lindsay, A. N., Voorhess, M. L., & MacGillivray, M. H. (1983, Apr). Multicystic ovaries in primary hypothyroidism. *Obstetrics and Gynecology, 61*(4), 433-437.

London, R. S., et al. (1984). The effect of alpha-tocopherol on premenstrual symptomatology: A double blind study. II. Endocrine correlates. *The Journal of the American College of Nutrition, 3*(4), 351-356.

Macfarlane, B. J., et al. (1990, May). Effect of traditional oriental soy products on iron absorption. *The American Journal of Clinical Nutrition, 51*(5), 873-880.

Mäenpää, J., & Liewendahl, K. (1980, Mar). Peripheral insensitivity to thyroid hormones in a euthyroid girl with goitre. *Archives of Disease in Childhood, 55*(3), 207-212.

Mandel, S. J., Larsen, P. R., Seely, E. W., & Brent, G. A. (1990, Jul). Increased need for thyroxine during pregnancy in women with primary hypothyroidism. *New England Journal of Medicine, 323*(2), 91-96.

Mattes, J. A., & Gittelman R. (1981, Jun). Effects of artificial food colorings in children with hyperactive symptoms. *Archives of General Psychiatry, 38*(6), 714-718.

Matthew, R. J., & Wilson, W. H. (1990, Jul). Behavioral and cerebrovascular effects of caffeine in patients with anxiety disorders. *Acta Psychiatrica Scandinavica, 82*(1), 17-22.

McCabe, D., Lisy, K., Lockwood, C., & Colbeck, M. (2017, Feb). The impact of essential fatty acid, B vitamins, vitamin C, magnesium and zinc supplementation on stress levels in women: A systematic review. *JBI Database of Systematic Reviews and Implementation Reports, 15*(2):402-453.

McCann, D. et al. (2007, Nov 3). Food additives and hyperactive behavior in 3-year-old and 8/9-year-old children in the community: A randomized, double-blinded, placebo-controlled trial. *Lancet, 370*(9598), 1560-1567.

McLeod, M. N., Gaynes, B., N., & Golden, R., N. (1999, Apr). Chromium potentiation of antidepressant pharmacotherapy for dysthymic disorder in 5 patients. *The Journal of Clinical Psychiatry, 60*(4), 237-240.

McManamy, M. C., & Schube, P. G. (1936). Caffeine intoxication: Report of a case the symptoms of which amounted to a psychosis. *New England Journal of Medicine, 215*, 616-620.

McNamara, R. K., Jandacek, R., Tso, P., Blom, T. J., Welge, J. A., Strawn, J. R., Adler, C. M., Strakowski, S. M., & DelBello, M. P. (2016, Jun). Adolescents with or at ultra-high risk for bipolar disorder exhibit erythrocyte docosahexaenoic acid and eicosapentaenoic acid deficits: A candidate prodromal risk biomarker. *Early Intervention in Psychiatry, 10*(3), 203-211.

Messamore, E., & McNamara, R. K. (2016). Detection and treatment of omega-3 fatty acid deficiency in psychiatric practice: Rationale and implementation. *Lipids in Health and Disease, 15*, 25.

Mikkelsen, K., Stojanovska, L., Prakash, M., & Apostolopoulos, V. (2017, Feb). The effects of vitamin B on the immune/cytokine network and their involvement in depression. *Maturitas, 96*, 58-71.

Milner, G. (1963, Mar). Ascorbic acid in chronic psychiatric patients - a controlled trial. *British Journal of Psychiatry, 109*(459), 294-299.

Möhler, H., et al. (1979, Apr 5). Nicotinamide is a brain constituent with benzodiazepine-like actions. *Nature, 278*(5704), 563-565.

Møller, S. E., Kirk, L., & Fremming, K. H. (1976, Sep 17). Plasma amino acids as an index for subgroups in manic depressive psychosis: Correlation to effect of tryptophan. *Psychopharmacology, 49*(2), 205-213.

Mortola, J. F., Liu, J. H., Gillin, J. C., Rasmussen, D. D., & Yen, S. S. (1987, Nov). Pulsatile rhythms of adrenocorticotropin (ACTH) and cortisol in women with endogenous depression: Evidence for increased ACTH pulse frequency. *Journal of Clinical Endocrinology and Metabolism, 65*(5), 962-968.

Mouret, J., et al. (1988, Dec 24-31). Treatment of narcolepsy with L-tyrosine. *Lancet, 2*(8626-8627), 1458-1459.

Murray, M. J., & Stein N. (1968, Mar 23). A gastric factor promoting iron absorption. *Lancet, 1*(7543), 614-616.

Nardi, A. E., et al. (2008). A caffeine challenge test in panic disorder patients, their healthy first-degree relatives, and healthy controls. *Depression and Anxiety, 25*(10), 847-853.

Nehlig, A., Daval, J. L., & Debry, G. (1992, May-Aug). Caffeine and the central nervous system: Mechanisms of action, biochemical, metabolic and psychostimulant effects. *Brain Research Reviews, 17*(2):139-70.

Nemets, B., Stahl, Z., & Belmaker, R. H. (2002, Mar). Addition of omega-3 fatty acid to maintenance medication treatment for recurrent unipolar depressive disorder. *American Journal of Psychiatry, 159*(3), 477-479.

Nemets, H., et al. (2006, Jun). Omega-3 treatment of childhood depression: A controlled, double-blind pilot study. *American Journal of Psychiatry, 163*(6), 1098-1100.

Neumeister, A., et al. (2004, Aug). Neural and behavioral responses to tryptophan depletion in unmedicated patients with remitted major depression disorder and controls. *Archives of General Psychiatry, 61*(8), 765-773.

Neylan, T. C. (1995). Treatment of sleep disturbances in depressed patients. *Journal of Clinical Psychiatry, 56*(Suppl 2), 56-61.

Nicar, M. J., & Pak, C. Y. (1985, Aug). Calcium bioavailability from calcium carbonate and calcium citrate. *The Journal of Clinical Endocrinology & Metabolism, 61*(2), 391-393.

NIH Consensus Development Conference. (1982). Defined diets and childhood hyperactivity. *Clinical Pediatrics, 21,* 627-630.

Nishihara, K., & Mori, K. (1996, Oct). The differences of self-ratings of sleep quality associated with epinephrine and wake time during 4-hour sleep. *Psychiatry and Clinical Neuroscience, 50*(5), 277-283.

O'Connell, M. B., et al. (2005, Jul). Effects of proton pump inhibitors on calcium carbonate absorption in women: A randomized crossover trial. *The American Journal of Medicine, 118*(7), 778-781.

O'Connor, P. J., Morgan, W. P., Raglin, J. S., Barksdale, C. M., & Kalin, N. H. (1989). Mood state and salivary cortisol levels following overtraining in female swimmers. *Psychoneuroendocrinology, 14*(4), 303-10.

Ohta, T., et al. (1990). Treatment of adolescent patients with sleep-wake schedule disturbances who complain of non-attendance at school. *Progress in Clinical and Biological Research, 341B,* 65-72.

Ohta, T., et al. (1991, Mar). Treatment of persistent sleep-wake schedule disorders in adolescents and vitamin B12. *The Japanese Journal of Psychiatry and Neurology, 45*(1), 167-168.

Osmond, H., & Hoffer, A. (1962, Feb 10). Massive niacin treatment in schizophrenia. *Lancet, 1*(7224), 316-319.

Palatnik, A., et al. (2001, Jun). Double-blind, controlled, crossover trial of inositol verses fluvoxamine for the treatment of panic disorder. *Journal of Clinical Psychopharmacology, 21*(3), 335-339.

Pearsall, R., Smith, D. J., Pelosi, A., & Geddes, J. (2014, Apr 21). Exercise therapy in adults with serious mental illness: A systematic review and meta-analysis. *BMC Psychiatry, 14,* 117.

Peet, M., et al. (2001, Apr 30). Two double-blind placebo-controlled pilot studies of eicosapentaenoic acid in the treatment of schizophrenia. *Schizophrenia Research, 49*(3), 243-251.

Peet, M., et al. (2002, Oct). A dose-ranging study of the effects of ethyl-eicosapentaenoate in patients with ongoing depression despite apparently adequate treatment with standard drugs. *Archives of General Psychiatry, 59*(10), 913-919.

Penland, J. G., & Johnson, P. E. (1993, May). Dietary calcium and manganese effects on menstrual cycle symptoms. *American Journal of Obstetrics and Gynecology, 168*(5), 1417-1423.

Petrie, K., Conaglen, J. V., Thompson, L, & Chamberlain, K. (1989, Mar 18). Effect of melatonin on jet lag after long haul flights. *The British Medical Journal, 298*(6675), 705-707.

Pincomb, G. A., Lovallo, W. R., Passey, R. B., Brackett, D. J., & Wilson, M. F. (1987). Caffeine enhances the physiological response to occupational stress in medical students. *Health Psychology, 6*(2), 101-112.

Pollock, M. A., et al. (2001, Oct 20). Thyroxine treatment in patients with symptoms of hypothyroidism but thyroid function tests within the reference range: Randomised double blind placebo controlled crossover trial. *BMJ, 323*(7318), 891-895.

Pontifex, M. B., et al. (2013, Mar). Exercise improves behavioral, neurocognitive, and scholastic performance in children with attention-deficit/hyperactivity disorder. *Journal of Pediatrics, 162*(3), 543-51. doi: 10.1016/j.jpeds.2012.08.036. Epub 2012 Oct 17.

Popper, C. W. (2001, Dec). Do vitamins or minerals (apart from lithium) have mood-stabilizing effects? *The Journal of Clinical Psychiatry, 62*(12), 933-935.

Prinz, R. J., Roberts, W. A., & Hantman, E. (1980, Dec). Dietary correlates of hyperactive behavior in children. *Journal of Consulting and Clinical Psychology, 48*(6), 760-769.

Prior, J. C., Vigna, Y., Sciarretta, D., Alojado, N., & Schulzer, M. (1987, Mar). Conditioning exercise decreases premenstrual symptoms: A prospective, controlled 6-month trial. *Fertility and Sterility, 47*(3), 402-408.

Prousky, J. E. (2004). Niacinamide's potent role in alleviating anxiety with its benzodiazepine-like properties: A case report. *Journal of Orthomolecular Medicine, 19*(2), 104-110.

Puri, B. K., et al. (2001, Oct). Eicosapentaenoic acid in treatment-resistant depression associated with symptom remission, structural brain changes and reduced neuronal phospholipid turnover. *International Journal of Clinical Practice, 55*(8), 560-563.

Puri, B. K., & Martins, J. G. (2014, May). Which polyunsaturated fatty acids are active in children with attention-deficit hyperactivity disorder receiving PUFA supplementation? A fatty acid validated meta-regression analysis of randomized

controlled trials. *Prostaglandins Leukot Essent Fatty Acids, 90*(5), 179-189.

Quaranta, S., et al. (2007). Pilot study of the efficacy and safety of a modified-release magnesium 250 mg tablet (Sincromag) for the treatment of premenstrual syndrome. *Clinical Drug Investigation, 27*(1), 51-58.

Rabinowitch, I. M. (1949, Sep). Achlorhydria and its clinical significance in diabetes mellitus. *American Journal of Digestive Disorders, 16*(9), 322-32.

Recker, R. R. (1985, Jul). Calcium absorption and achlorhydria. *New England Journal of Medicine, 313*(2), 70-73.

Refetoff, S. (1992, Jul). Clinical and genetic aspects of resistance to thyroid hormone. *Endocrinologist, 2*(4), 261-272.

Reifler, B. V. (1996). Depression, anxiety, and sleep disturbances. *International Psychogeriatrics, 8*(Suppl 3), 415-418.

Richardson, A. J., & Puri, B. K. (2002, Feb). A randomized double-blind, placebo-controlled study of the effects of supplementation with highly unsaturated fatty acids on ADHD-related symptoms in children with specific learning difficulties. *Progress in Neuro-Psychopharmacology & Biological Psychiatry, 26*(2), 233-239.

Rihs, M., Muller, C., & Baumann, P. (1996). Caffeine consumption in hospitalized psychiatric patients. *European Archives of Psychiatry and Clinical Neuroscience, 246*(2), 83-92.

Rippere, V. (1982, Jun). Placebo-controlled tests of chemical food additives: Are they valid? *Medical Hypotheses, 7*(6), 819-823.

Roca, D. J., Schiller, G. D., & Farb, D. H. (1988, May). Chronic caffeine or theophylline exposure reduces gamma-aminobutyric acid/benzodiazepine receptor site interactions. *Molecular Pharmacology, 33*(5), 481-485.

Roca, M., Kohls, E., Gili, M., Watkins, E., Owens, M., Hegerl, U., van Grootheest, G., Bot, M., Cabout, M., Brouwer, I. A., Visser,

M., & Penninx, B. W., MooDFOOD Prevention Trial Investigators. (2016, Jun 8). Prevention of depression through nutritional strategies in high-risk persons: Rationale and design of the MooDFOOD prevention trial. *BMC Psychiatry, 16*, 192.

Rossignol, A. M. (1985, Nov). Caffeine-containing beverages and premenstrual syndrome in young women. *American Journal of Public Health, 75*(11), 1335-1337.

Rossignol, A. M., & Bonnlander, H. (1990, Sep). Caffeine-containing beverages, total fluid consumption, and premenstrual syndrome. *American Journal of Public Health, 80*(9), 1106-1110.

Rowe, A. H. (1959, Jan-Feb). Allergic fatigue and toxemia. *Annals of Allergy, Asthma & Immunology, 17*(1), 9-18.

Rowe, K. S., & Rowe, K. J. (1994, Nov). Synthetic food coloring and behavior: A dose response effect in a double-blind, placebo-controlled, repeated-measures study. *Journal of Pediatrics, 125*(5 Pt 1), 691-698.

Roy-Byrne, P. P., & Uhde, T. W. (1988, Feb). Exogenous factors in panic disorder: Clinical and research implications. *Journal of Clinical Psychiatry, 49*(2), 56-61.

Rudin, D. O. (1981, Sep). The major psychoses and neuroses as omega-3 essential fatty acid deficiency syndrome: Substrate pellagra. *Biological Psychiatry, 16*(9), 837-850.

Russel, R. M., Krasinski, S. D., & Samloff, M. (1984). Correction of impaired folic acid (Pte Glu) absorption by orally administered HCI in subjects with gastric atrophy. *The American Journal of Clinical Nutrition, 39*, 656.

Salzman, L. K. (1976, Aug). Allergy testing, psychological assessment and dietary treatment of the hyperactive child syndrome. *Medical Journal of Australia, 2*(7), 248-251.

Schuette, S., Lashner, B. A., & Janghorbani, M. (1994, Sep-Oct). Bioavailability of Mg diglycinate vs MgO in patients with ileal resection. *JPEN Journal of Parenter Enteral Nutr, 18*(5), 430-435.

Searle, G. F. (1994, Aug). The effect of dietary caffeine manipulation on blood caffeine, sleep and disturbed behavior. *Journal of Intellectual Disability Research, 38*(Pt 4), 383-391.

Serfaty-Lacrosniere, C., et al. (1995, Aug). Hypochlorhydria from short-term omeprazole treatment does not inhibit intestinal absorption of calcium, phosphorus, magnesium or zinc from food in humans. *The Journal of the American College of Nutrition, 14*(4), 364-368.

Sharp, G. S., & Fister, H. W. (1967). The diagnosis and treatment of achlorhydria: A ten-year study. *Journal of American Geriatric Society, 15*, 786-791.

Shaw, Jr., D. L., Chesney, M. A., Tullis, I. F., & Agersborg, H. P. (1962, Jun). Management of fatigue: A physiologic approach. *The American Journal of Medical Sciences, 243*, 758-769.

Sheehan, D. V., Ballenger, J., & Jacobsen, G. (1980, Jan). Treatment of endogenous anxiety and phobic, hysterical and hypochondriacal symptoms. *Archives of General Psychiatry, 37*(1), 51-59.

Sherwood, R. A., Rocks, B. F., Stewart, A., & Saxton, R. S. (1986, Nov). Magnesium and the premenstrual syndrome. *Annals of Clinical Biochemistry, 23*(Pt 6), 667-670.

Silva, A. P., Prado, S. O. S., Scardovelli, T. A., Boschi, S. R. M. S., Campos, L. C., & Frère, A. F. (2015, Mar 24). Measurement of the effect of physical exercise on the concentration of individuals with ADHD. *PLoS One, 10*(3), e0122119. doi: 10.1371/journal.pone.0122119.

Silverman, K., Evans, S. M., Strain, E. C., & Griffiths, R. R. (1992, Oct 15). Withdrawal syndrome after the double-blind cessation of caffeine consumption. *New England Journal of Medicine, 327*(16), 1109-1114.

Sinn, N., & Bryan, J. (2007, Apr). Effect of supplementation with polyunsaturated fatty acids and micronutrients on learning and behavior problems associated with child ADHD. *Journal of Developmental and Behavioral Pediatrics, 28*(2), 82-91.

Skinner, G. R., et al. (1997, June 14). Thyroxine should be tried in clinically hypothyroid but biochemically euthyroid patients. *BMJ, 314*(7096), 1764.

Skinner, G. R. B., et al. (2000, Jun). Clinical response to thyroxine sodium in clinically hypothyroid but biochemically euthyroid patients *Journal of Nutritional and Environmental Medicine, 10*(2), 115-125.

Smith, G. A. (1988, Sep). Caffeine reduction as an adjunct to anxiety management. *British Journal of Clinical Psychology, 27*(Pt 3), 265-266.

Sorgi, P. J., Hallowell, E. M., Hutchins, H. L., & Sears, B. (2007, Jul 13). Effects of an open-label pilot study with high-dose EPA/DHA concentrates on plasma phospholipids and behavior in children with attention deficit hyperactivity disorder. *Nutrition Journal, 6*, 16.

Speer, F. (1958). The allergic tension-fatigue syndrome in children. *International Archives of Allergy and Applied Immunology, 12*(3-4), 207-214.

Stancer, H. C., & Persad, E. (1982, Mar). Treatment of intractable rapid-cycling manic-depressive disorder with levothyroxine. *Archives of General Psychiatry, 39*(3), 311-312.

Steinberg, S., Annable, L., Young, S. N., & Liyange, N. (1999, Feb). A placebo-controlled clinical trial of L-tryptophan in premenstrual dysphoria. *Biological Psychiatry, 45*(3), 313-320.

Stevens, L. J., et al. (1995, Oct). Essential fatty acid metabolism in boys with attention-deficit hyperactivity disorder. *The American Journal of Clinical Nutrition, 62*(4), 761-768.

Stevenson, J., et al. (2014, May). Research review: The role of diet in the treatment of attention-deficit/hyperactivity disorder-and appraisal of the evidence on the efficacy and recommendations on design of future studies. *Journal of Child Psychology and Psychiatry, 55*(5), 416-427.

Stoffer, S. S. (1982, Aug). Menstrual disorders and mild thyroid insufficiency: Intriguing cases suggesting an association. *Postgraduate Medical Journal, 72*(2), 75-77, 80-82.

Stoll, A. L., et al. (1999, May). Omega 3 fatty acids in bipolar disorder: A preliminary double-blind, placebo-controlled trial. *Archives of General Psychiatry, 56*(5), 407-412.

Strachan, R. W., & Henderson, J. G. (1965, Jul). Psychiatric syndromes due to avitaminosis B12 with normal blood and marrow. *Q J Med, 34*(135), 303-317.

Sturniolo, G. C., et al. (1991, Aug). Inhibition of gastric acid secretion reduces zinc absorption in man. *The Journal of the American College of Nutrition, 10*(4), 372-375.

Swanson, J. M., & Kinsbourne, M. (1980, Mar). Food dyes impair performance of hyperactive children on a laboratory learning test. *Science, 207*(4438), 1485-1487.

Taylor, W. H. (1962). Proteinases of the stomach in health and disease. *Physiological Reviews, 42*, 519-553.

Terry, W. S., & Phifer, B. (1986, Nov). Caffeine and memory performance on the AVLT. *Journal of Clinical Psychology, 42*(6), 860-863.

Thomson, J., et al. (1982, Nov). The treatment of depression in general practice: A comparison of L-tryptophan, amitriptyline, and a combination of L-tryptophan and amitriptyline with placebo. *Psychological Medicine, 12*(4), 741-751.

Thys-Jacobs, S., Starkey, P., Bernstein, D., & Tian, J. (1998, Aug). Calcium carbonate and the premenstrual syndrome: Effects on premenstrual and menstrual symptoms. *American Journal of Obstetrics and Gynecology, 179*(2), 444-452.

Toft, A. D. (1999, Feb 11). Thyroid hormone replacement - one hormone or two? *New England Journal of Medicine, 340*(6), 469-470.

Tondo, L., & Rudas, N. (1991, Aug). The course of a seasonal bipolar disorder influenced by caffeine. *Journal of Affective Disorders, 22*(4), 249-251.

Vagenakis, A. G., et al. (1975, Oct 2). Recovery of pituitary thyrotropic function after withdrawal of prolonged thyroid-suppression therapy. *New England Journal of Medicine, 293*(14), 681-684.

van Pragg, H. M. (1980, Jan-Feb). Central monoamine metabolism in depression II: Catecholamines and related compounds. *Comprehensive Psychiatry, 21*(1), 44-54.

Vescovi, P. P., et al. (1987). Nicotinic acid effectiveness in the treatment of benzodiazepine withdrawal. *Current Therapeutic Research, 41,* 429-433.

Vikkunen, M. (1986, May). Reactive hypoglycemic tendency among habitually violent offenders. *Nutrition Review, 44*(Suppl), 94-103.

Vollrath, M., Wicki, W., & Angst, J. (1989). The Zurich study VIII: Insomnia: association with depression, anxiety, somatic syndromes, and course insomnia. *European Archives of Psychiatry and Neurological Sciences, 239*(2), 113-124.

Walker, A. F., et al. (1998, Nov). Magnesium supplementation alleviates premenstrual symptoms of fluid retention. *Journal of Women's Health, 7*(9), 1157-1165.

Weiss, B., et al. (1980, Mar 28). Behavioral responses to artificial food colors. *Science, 207*(4438), 1487-1489.

Weissman, M. M. (1987). Epidemiology of depression: Frequency, risk groups, and risk factors. In *Perspectives on Depressive Disorders: A Review of Recent Research* (pp. 1-22). Rockville, MD: National Institute of Mental Health.

Wikland, B., Löwhagen, T., & Sandberg, P. O. (2001, Mar 24). Fine-needle aspiration cytology of the thyroid in chronic fatigue. *Lancet, 357*(9260). 956-957.

Williams, J. I., Cram, D. M., Tausig, F. T., & Webster, E. (1978, Jun). Relative effects of drugs and diet on hyperactive behaviors: An experimental study. *Pediatrics, 61*(6), 811-817.

Williams, M. J., Harris, R. I., & Dean, B. C. (1985). Controlled trial of pyridoxine in the premenstrual syndrome. *Journal of International Medical Research, 13*(3), 174-179.

Wittenborn, J. R., Weber, E. S., & Brown, M. (1973, Mar). Niacin in the long-term treatment of schizophrenia. *Archives of General Psychiatry, 28*(3), 308-315.

Wozniak, J., et al. (2007, May-Jun). Omega-3 fatty acid monotherapy for pediatric bipolar disorder: A prospective open-label trial. *European Neuropsychopharmacology, 17*(6-7), 440-447.

Wozniak, J., et al. (2015, Nov). A randomized clinical trial of high eicosapentaenoic acid omega-3 fatty acids and inositol as monotherapy and in combination in the treatment of pediatric bipolar spectrum disorders: A pilot study. *The Journal of Clinical Psychiatry, 76*(11), 1548-1555.

Wright, J. V., & Lenard, L. (2001). *Why stomach acid is good for you: Natural relief from heartburn, indigestion, reflux and GERD.* Lanham, MD: M. Evans & Company.

Wu, X., Ohinmaa, A., & Veugelers, P. J. (2016, Dec 2). The influence of health behaviours in childhood on attention deficit and hyperactivity disorder in adolescence. *Nutrients, 8*(12), pii: E788.

Yaryura-Tobias, J. A., & Bhagavan, H. N. (1977, Nov). L-Tryptophan in obsessive-compulsive disorders. *American Journal of Psychiatry, 134*(11), 1298-1299.

Ylöstalo, P., Kujala, P., & Kontula, K. (1980). Amenorrhea with low normal thyroid function and thyroxine treatment. *International Journal of Gynecology & Obstetrics, 18*(3), 176-180.